FLY

An empty nester's quest for the holy grail of
life, love and longevity

By Christopher Saye

Cover design by Sunil Sebastian
Author photo by Suki Zoë
Edited by Eva Marie Everson and Phil Goddard

Hardcover ISBN: 978-1-7376456-0-3
Paperback ISBN: 978-1-7376456-1-0
eBook ISBN: 978-1-7376456-2-7

This work depicts actual events in the life of the author as truthfully as recollection permits. All persons within are actual individuals. The names of some individuals have been changed to respect their privacy.

For those who have pushed me to be more

TABLE OF CONTENTS

Prologue 7

The Start 9

Homeless 15

Okinawa Part I 19

Okinawa Part II 38

Life and Death 52

Costa Rica 74

Hope 106

Sardinia 122

Halftime 136

Ikaria 153

Preparing for Take-Off 166

Epilogue 185

PROLOGUE

I began writing this book as a travelogue, simply documenting what had been a year of travels around the world with my wife, Galina, to mark our transition to becoming 'empty nesters'. As I started to write I didn't know how the book was going to end nor did I know what would become of our relationship at this critical juncture in life.

Writing can be cathartic and this book certainly was for me. The book evolved from a simple travelogue about longevity hotspots to a search for my core values and much more.

My hope is that, through this book, readers can look honestly at their lives, whether it be their own lives as individuals or a life shared with someone else, and get in touch with their own core values. This is the path to living a life of integrity. We all have freedom to choose how we respond to life's circumstances and the power to create the life we want.

THE START

"YOU HAVE TO MEET THIS GIRL." Nurtaza then proceeded to almost physically drag me from my seat at the conference table. Our small team of auditors occupied our client's board room, located in a partially renovated Soviet-style office on Lenin Avenue. It was April 1995, and I was an audit manager with the accounting firm Arthur Andersen in Almaty, Kazakhstan, responsible for overseeing the audit of the financial statements of a Canadian oil company.

Nurtaza, one of our senior Kazakh employees, led the small team of accountants working at the client's office, where he had already spent a few days and had met Galina, the charming and stunningly beautiful personal assistant to the finance director. I had shown up for a few hours to review files and meet the client.

Nurtaza had known me since I arrived in Almaty the previous year, and somehow had a feeling this girl was one I needed to meet. Neither Galina nor I knew how this introduction would change our lives.

The choir of angels seemed to start singing from the moment I opened the door; their tune rose to a crescendo as I extended my hand to greet the girl with whom I felt an immediate connection. It was love at first sight for the both of us, and nothing could stop our hearts from connecting as we were drawn together by a force that I had never before—and never since—experienced.

I can't remember how it all happened, but within seconds we agreed to drive up to the mountains together after work, Nurtaza tagging along. Dinner followed at a Chinese restaurant in town. Later that night, I said goodbye with a shy handshake.

That was the last time a handshake would suffice.

We were both in our mid-twenties and not particularly looking for a long-term relationship, yet neither of us could deny what we felt for each other. Our relationship grew and we married almost two years after that first meeting.

Galina had given birth to Natasha six years earlier when she was nineteen and still in university, pretty much standard operating procedure for girls growing up in the villages of Siberia, where Galina was born and raised. Birth control was neither spoken about nor readily available in the Soviet Union. Galina's mother had raised Natasha from birth, but Galina suddenly became the primary caregiver when her mother passed away from stomach cancer at the age of fifty-four, just a few weeks before we met.

So, Galina and I started our relationship from the get-go with one child and in time I formally adopted Natasha. In the meantime we also produced two boys, Nicholas in 1998 and Marcus in 2000.

The decade following the fall of the Soviet Union in 1991 was a fascinating time of massive change and economic activity in Russia, and all the former Soviet republics, including Kazakhstan. I initially came to Moscow in 1992, moving there with Arthur Andersen as a young accountant looking for adventure. I had kind of fallen into accounting by default during university, after drifting away from my passions and letting the fear of not being gainfully employed get the most of me. Consequently, I was not particularly happy working as an auditor in Arthur Andersen's Houston office after graduation. About two years into my stint with the firm, the opportunity came to move to Russia, the new "wild west" with it having been a mostly closed society for almost seventy years. I jumped at the chance to dive into the unknown.

I lived and worked in Moscow for about two years, and then moved to Almaty, which at the time was the capital of the newly independent country of Kazakhstan. I met Galina (and Natasha) there the following year and quickly became fluent in Russian.

We spent the first four years of our married life living in Kazakhstan and Azerbaijan before then moving to Moscow. By this time I was a partner with Arthur Andersen, having moved up the ranks quite efficiently in the dynamic and opportunity-rich business environment of the post-Soviet Union. It is highly unlikely that I would have had such career progression had I stayed working in Houston. Despite my fast rise to partnership, Arthur Andersen collapsed in 2002 after the fall of Enron, one of several big corporate accounting scandals that unfolded at the turn of the century.

At this point, however, my fluency in Russian allowed me to take advantage of some unique professional opportunities. In the early 2000s commodity prices boomed and money sloshed around the world like water, especially in Russia. Salaries were high and bonuses big for many professionals—Russian and expatriates alike—who worked in Russia at that time. After Arthur Andersen collapsed, I spent the next five years working in senior finance roles inside two large Russian companies: an aluminum producer and a large oil company, both of which proved to be financially lucrative.

And then, I suddenly felt rich, thanks primarily to the value of shares I had been awarded by my employer. My role in the company had come to an obvious pause point and cashing in my shares felt like the right thing to do. By this time we had spent six consecutive years living in Moscow, which allowed Natasha to go through middle and high school in one location. Galina and I agreed this kind of stability was important for a child, but once she graduated from high school, we were ready for a move.

We wanted to create unique life and education experiences for our boys as they went through school. With Nicholas and Marcus being nine and eleven years younger than Natasha, respectively, we still had over a decade to dedicate to educating the boys. My work in Russia had been sufficiently lucrative so that I no longer felt the need to work (for money at least) for the foreseeable future. So we moved to my hometown in Texas where my parents still lived. We spent two years in Houston before moving to Slovenia, where I took a job advising the founder of an international school network headquartered in Ljubljana. The boys, of course, attended school in both Texas and Slovenia, and from there we had the chance to spend one winter term in Phuket, Thailand, where they attended the sister school of their school in Slovenia.

By this time we were starting to focus on a location where we wanted the boys to attend high school. Singapore ticked many boxes, being a safe, global hub with strong academic standards. The United World College of Southeast Asia really resonated with us in terms of its mission to be a force to unite people, nations, and cultures. After all, our family was a product of the Cold War coming to an end and the re-unification, even if only for a short time, of the East with the West.

Having lived in Kazakhstan, Azerbaijan, Russia, Texas, Slovenia, and Thailand, it was time to move to Singapore where we would finish out our childrearing years. We had moved most of our furniture and home furnishings to Slovenia from Texas, but all this moving stuff around was both difficult and expensive. We decided to pack up a household of furniture, pictures, dishes, and similar items, and put them into long-term storage in Slovenia, before making the move to Asia. We told the owner of the storage unit that we would probably ship all or most of our things out to Singapore, but years later we were still sending him an annual storage fee.

Before moving to Singapore, however, we got a bit side-tracked when we heard about a new school concept in Bali, Indonesia. Green School was made almost entirely from bamboo, with open classrooms. Students get their hands dirty in food-producing gardens and learn science in rice fields. This was an opportunity too unique to pass up; we took a slight detour from Slovenia to Indonesia and spent a year in Bali for the boys to attend Green School.

Bali was an amazing family experience. We lived in a beautiful bamboo house, and the boys rode bikes through the jungle each morning to school. This was our transition to Singapore, where we moved with the clear intent of living for six years so that both boys could be in one place throughout high school.

Just before leaving Bali for Singapore, John Hardy, Green Schools's co-founder, asked me to help him manage his personal finances and help oversee the school on his behalf. My fiduciary role with John and Green School continued to develop over the years while we lived in Singapore. Green School grew and six years later, I had finally put together a management team and group of investors designed to launch new Green Schools around the world.

By now Galina and I had accomplished our primary mission together. Both boys had loved their school experiences at United World College in Singapore, and their education there set them up very well to pursue their dreams. Nicholas was already studying design at IE University in Spain, and Marcus was on track to study mechanical engineering at Imperial College London.

This brought us to the beginning of a new stage in life. We

were now officially "empty nesters." For the first time in our relationship there was no child with us. We had started with one, grown to two, then three, then shrank back to two, then one and now . . . we had none. Virtually all our big life decisions thus far had been made with the upbringing and education of our children as the determining factor. They were the glue that held us together and we were left with one question: *what now*?

HOMELESS

"I've learned that home isn't a place, it's a feeling."
- Cecelia Ahern (Love, Rosie)

TWELVE DAYS AFTER MARCUS GRADUATED from high school in Singapore, the city-state in Southeast Asia that we, as a family, had called home for the past six years, Galina and I held one-way tickets for Taipei, the capital of Taiwan. The lease on our apartment had expired and we had put most of our personal belongings in storage. The final boxes were added only a few hours before we left for the airport.

We had spent those six years in Singapore for the primary purpose of educating our sons. Now that both had finished school, we were free from the bonds of school, activities, and friends which are a normal part of raising children. Our children had been a strong bond, the *glue* which held us together for over twenty years. That glue was now gone, and we had known for some time that we would need to find a new sense of purpose, either together as a couple or as individuals—or both.

By the time we were boarding our flight to Taiwan, Natasha was married with children of her own, and Nicholas had graduated from high school in Singapore two years prior. With Marcus now also finished with school, we were together as a couple in a way we had never been.

Taiwan was to be our hopping-off spot—a place to store some luggage for our onward journey to the US, while we spent time in Okinawa, Japan, for the next two months. Okinawa is one of the

"Blue Zones," five regions around the world identified by National Geographic explorer and author Dan Buettner, where people live longer than average. Dan wrote *The Blue Zones*[i] about five places he and his team had identified with a high concentration of healthy centenarians: Okinawa, Japan, the isolated Nicoya Peninsula in Costa Rica, the Italian island of Sardinia, a Greek island named Ikaria, and Loma Linda, California.

Ever since her mother died from cancer, Galina had developed a keen interest in all things to do with health and wellness, so a book about longevity naturally attracted her attention. And since she was a young girl growing up in Siberia, she had dreamed of traveling. She had turned that dream into reality even before we met, and over the years took the lead in planning family vacations. We traveled to many countries on short trips, often without the children, including Iran, Cuba, and Lebanon.

The combination of wellness, longevity, and travel appealed to her so much that, about a year prior to Marcus's graduation, she proposed we travel to each of the Blue Zones. But this would not be just a sightseeing visit. She wanted to really *experience* each of these places and spend enough time in each location to become immersed. This would, of course, be a major disruption, but Galina felt this was exactly what we needed to do at this critical stage in life and I agreed.

Many marriages fall apart once kids leave the house, and we had already begun sensing for ourselves how this can happen. Each partner gets settled into their own routine and life carries on. Boredom sets in and splitting up can seem an obvious and convenient route to happiness. Each partner knows the other one all too well and there is nothing new to be learned, so why not start over anew with someone else? After all, we were not yet fifty, so we had plenty of time to have a run with another partner, if nothing more than for a change of scenery.

But, did one, or both, of us want to leave the marriage? What would be the driving forces, or values, which would determine how we would live out the rest of our lives? We needed to answer these questions both for ourselves as individuals, and as a couple.

This Blue Zone-inspired journey would be a disrupting life event, one that would be both interesting and educational, and one which would also give us the chance to spend enough time together to know how, or if, we would carry on as life partners. Could we discover some new *glue* for our relationship?

Galina had always told our children that if they wanted to test a serious relationship, they should travel together. Travel takes people out of their comfort zones and routines, and brings out the real person. You get to see how you and your travel partner react to new situations, challenges, and environments. We were now about to apply that same advice to our own relationship.

With tickets in hand, we boarded an overnight flight from Singapore to Taipei. We did not yet have tickets for a flight to Okinawa, nor did we know how long we would be able to stay. Our aim was to spend about two months in Okinawa, but Natasha, who lived in Texas, was pregnant with her third child, due to be born in just under two months. We had not been with her for the birth of her first two children (our first grandchildren), and we really *did* want to be present the third time around.

Although we had good "excuses" for missing the prior births (attending to responsibilities related to our own children), we no longer had any valid excuse not to be with her for this one. Truth be told, since the birth of our first grandchild, when we were both just forty-three, there was a bit of denial of us actually *being* grandparents, and that likely played a factor in how we managed to avoid the first two births. But with our youngest child now fully grown, we could stop denying and now fully embrace our more "mature" status.

We had agreed between ourselves and Natasha that we would make it a priority to get back in time for her delivery, and if this meant cutting our time in Okinawa short, so be it. But first we needed to *get* to Okinawa and, other than by Tokyo which is much farther north, Taipei had the best flight connections.

We booked ourselves into a small hotel located in the top few floors of some sort of combined apartment/office/industrial warehouse in downtown Taipei, and immediately set out to look for a storage unit we could rent for about two months. My office in Singapore had prearranged a unit not too far from the city center. We arrived with four suitcases which we were not going to need in Okinawa (we intended to travel light) and met the office manager. She didn't speak a word of English and our storage contract was all in Mandarin, but I dutifully signed all the papers, not knowing at all what I was signing, then paid whatever she asked me to pay.

As we closed the door to the storage unit, less than half the size of our unit in Singapore, we started to count how many places held our belongings. There were now five with our "stuff" spread around the world in various storage units: Singapore and Taiwan, the homes of my parents in Texas and my sister in England, while most of our furniture and home furnishing remained in storage in Slovenia. We were now officially "homeless." In Russia, the government assigns an official status to someone who does not have a permanent address, and there is even an acronym for it – "BOMZh" – which, to me, sounds suspiciously like the word "bum." We were now BOMZh – and while there was a certain amount of excitement related to the freedom which would come with our upcoming travel, we both also felt a sense of insecurity and loss. We, and our stuff, were all over the place, but where was home?

OKINAWA PART I

"Agriculture is the most healthful, most useful and most noble employment of man."
- Widely attributed to George Washington

WE ALL WANT TO FEEL SIGNIFICANT in life and some of us, I believe, are simply born with a stronger sense of significance than others. One's self-worth is then built, or broken down, from this inborn state during childhood, adolescence, and into adulthood. In my experience, many people who achieve a lot in life, and arguably many so-called "over-achievers," do so from a place of wanting to feel significant and to prove their sense of self-worth.

When I look back on the time leading up to our departure from Singapore to our first Blue Zone location, Okinawa, I can see that I was struggling with the fear of losing significance. I knew that one of my primary purposes in life, if not my main purpose, was to father children. As humans, irrespective of whether one believes we are simply evolved animals or creatures made in the image of God (or some of both), at the most basic level it is our purpose to procreate. Of course, in this modern era, we all want to be self-actualized and live full lives according to our higher selves, but inside us all there is still a coded, hard-wired purpose to pass on our genes. And while some fathers may be content to simply have provided the seed to create a new life, my role as a father was important to me. From the moment I set my eyes on my firstborn I felt a strong sense of responsibility to be the best father I could be. I was intent to provide not only for his physical needs, but also to support his social, emotional, and intellectual development. I would be there for him and for his siblings in the years to come, and be an example of a loving, committed husband.

My own father had set a strong example for me and I was committed to follow in his footsteps. Being a father was a job that I took very seriously and one I believe I had done very well over the past two decades.

Before arriving in Okinawa, I had known for some time that this job was coming to an end. For years I had got up most mornings with the kids, served breakfast and saw them off to school. With our youngest now out of the house that job became obsolete. Fearing this impending crush to my significance, I had, in the preceding year or so, taken all kinds of steps, some rational and some not, to fill the impending void. I turned to my work and launched several rushed and "half-baked" business initiatives that ended up sucking my time, energy, and money. Perhaps more rationally, I also started a new side career as a life and business coach, which included taking a three-month coaching certification course.

But ultimately I had stretched myself too thin.

Galina had been picking up on this and tried to subtly, and at times not-so-subtly, remind me of where my priorities should be. When passive-aggressive attempts to get through didn't work (they rarely do), she would blow up emotionally, I would get defensive, and we would retreat to our own corners to cool down.

We'd then repeat the cycle.

With tension building in our relationship, and the self-imposed stress I had been putting on myself at work in my search for renewed significance, I came to Okinawa like a tightly wound clock. I needed to loosen up and, at the same time, start to accept the inevitable life changes that had already been set into motion.

From Taipei, we flew one-way to Okinawa's capital city, Naha. Aside from having read *The Blue Zones* book, including its chapter on Okinawa, we had done little research on the place. All we knew was that Okinawa was located somewhere in the Pacific Ocean, that it was part of Japan (although far to the south of Japan's mainland), it had something to do with World War II, and that the United States has a controversial military base there.

Okinawa is fairly remote, and closer geographically to China and Taiwan than to Japan. For centuries, this chain of more than one-hundred-fifty islands was its own distinct kingdom. They were previously dominated by the Chinese, then Japan, and after World War II, the US. Since 1972, Okinawa has been back under Japanese control, although the US continues to have an imposing military base on the island. Most people we met in Okinawa would, at some point, mention the presence of America's military on the island and, usually very tactfully, express some level of discontent.

While in Taiwan we booked our first week's accommodation in Okinawa on Airbnb, picking a cottage located in the small village of Chinen, about an hour away from the airport, on the southeast side of Okinawa's largest island, Okinawa Island. We were a five-minute walk from the sea. On this side of the island the sea is nicer to look at than to swim in because of the shallow—and jagged—coral and limestone, which extends several hundred meters out past the beach. Rather than swim we focused on taking walks around the town and small farming valleys, noting what grew there, and then buying and cooking what was sold in the shops. Lots of sweet potatoes (a staple in the local diet), mushrooms, bitter gourds, plus plenty of salad and greens. Ironically, there was not much sushi in Okinawa, nor, we noticed, did people greet each other with the typical Japanese bow. Although everyone spoke Japanese, culturally the island felt very different from Japan.

Prior to arriving, our Airbnb host (who apparently did not live in Okinawa and owned the place as a vacation home) had sent me an email to say that there was an elderly neighbor near the house who spoke English. He believed that Mr. Nagayoshi would be happy to meet us. We found his house and knocked on the door one afternoon to say hello. Mr. Nagayoshi, age eighty, was indeed excited to meet us and to get a chance to use his English. He told us that, despite reading and listening to English often, he hadn't actually spoken the language in years. We talked briefly while standing on his front porch, letting him warm up his spoken English, and he told us that he would pay us a visit soon.

Sure enough, Mr. Nagayoshi knocked on our door the next day. He brought along his camera and a few photo albums to show us his photo collection of birds and insects. Photography, we learned, is his hobby, one he took up when he retired at the age of sixty.

Mr. Nagayoshi attended the University of Hawaii in the 1960s as part of a scholarship program which sent young Okinawans to the US to study. This was, apparently, part of America's apology for bombing the hell out of Okinawa during the war. After university, he returned to Okinawa, and proceeded to have a long career teaching high school English. He remembers the war as a child, although he said that the main battles were fought on the other side of the island (only ten to twenty miles away), so he didn't suffer physically in any way, nor did he have any scaring memories. I found that to be incredible, because the Battle of Okinawa marked one the greatest losses of life on both sides during the War in the Pacific, with over 170,000 casualties.

I asked Mr. Nagayoshi if he knew that Okinawa was famous for people living long lives. He hadn't heard that. We spoke about things like community and diet, each of which appear to play roles in the longevity of people in all of the Blue Zones, but I couldn't get anything out of him which seemed to be the "secret sauce." He had just lived a simple life in this relatively simple environment, with no intention of living to be a centenarian.

That was the key takeaway from our conversation—he just lives. It's also a key takeaway from *The Blue Zones* book. People are born into an environment which, for historical reasons (or simply luck), sets them up well to live a long life. Galina and I were at the very beginning of our journey to discover what it was about these environments that made them so special.

And we were also at the very beginning of defining our new lives, from here on out. As we posed for photos together, smiling for Facebook in front of the beautiful turquoise waters which surround the islands of Okinawa, neither of us would admit out loud what we were feeling about our relationship, or acknowledge the painful questions we were asking ourselves.

Since arriving in Okinawa I was on the lookout for mugwort, a plant which grows like a weed and, according to *The Blue Zones,* has to some degree been part of the local diet over the years. Mugwort can be found in many parts of the world and it is revered for its medicinal properties in both Asia and Russia (where it is sold in pharmacies). Mr. Nagayoshi, however, didn't seem to know much about it - he thought it was just a weed.

We had also read in *The Blue Zones* about a centenarian woman in Okinawa who swore that the secret to her long life was drinking a daily cup of mugwort sake. (Sake is the Japanese version of vodka made from rice). We *attempted* to ask for mugwort sake in the shops and a local bar, but got rather confused looks from the shopkeepers before realizing that it must be a homemade brew. So we simply purchased some sake from the shop and made our own version of infused mugwort sake by shoving a bunch of mugwort leaves into the bottle. In our continued travels over the year ahead, we learned that moderate consumption of alcohol is a common factor in each of the Blue Zones we visited.

After having spent a few days in Chinen, the novelty of mugwort sake and our almost daily chats with Mr. Nagayoshi started to wear off, and we realized we needed to start making a plan for what we would do and where we would go in Okinawa. We were, after all, planning to spend up to two months there. What would we do with all this time? We had always placed a priority on exercise in our lives so this, we decided, was something to which we would allocate one or two hours a day. That still left a lot of time each day to keep our bodies and minds active.

To kick-start our adventure, Galina typed "volunteer opportunities in Okinawa" into Google and started to go through the search results. We quickly learned about "WWOOFing" and "WorkAway," two different online platforms which match up volunteer workers with "employers" who pay room and board in exchange for some sort of daily work. One day off for every six days worked is the norm, and workers are generally expected to work at least four hours a day.

In our younger years, neither of us had ever traveled by staying in youth hostels, backpacked across Europe, or done much in the way of hitchhiking. While we've always considered ourselves to be reasonably adventurous risk-takers, we also enjoyed comfort. I can easily convince myself that the cost of upgrading to business class on a flight is worth it, and we've been accused more than once by family members of having a penchant for fine dining. Yet here we were, considering working in exchange for our room and board.

WorkAway is a global site where people looking for labor advertise various kinds of work opportunities, ranging from babysitting to language training to toilet cleaning. You can read reviews of various hosts and it quickly becomes clear that the system can be abused by some unscrupulous types looking to take advantage of the young, naïve, or not-so-wealthy. But reviews written by previous guests do help to weed out the bad apples.

Japan—or at least Okinawa—did not actually offer many WorkAway opportunities, although we would come back to the site in the future. It turned out that Okinawa needed help in the agriculture sector.

"WWOOF" stands for Willing Workers on Organic Farms, and there a number of country-specific WWOOF websites which match hosts and workers for volunteer gigs all over the world. There is also a whole vocabulary which is part of this particular subculture. "WWOOFing" is the act of working on WWOOF-approved farms, and a "WWOOFer" is the worker.

We were about to become WWOOFers!

Searching the WWOOF Japan site, we came across the profile of a couple, a few years older than us, whose profile picture showed them in a field with two goats. In spite of my recently adopted plant-based (vegan) eating tendencies, I had always dreamt of owning goats so I latched onto the notion of volunteering at the Kyuna Dairy Farm. I assumed they got their dairy products, at least in part, from the cute goats in the profile photo. We messaged the farm's owners and explained that we had lots of free time in the coming weeks and we would love to come volunteer. Amazingly, we had a reply within a few hours saying that we could come as soon as the approaching weekend. This was perfect timing for us in terms of when our current (and only) Airbnb booking was to end, so we accepted and committed to stay for two weeks. We didn't have any other tangible options anyway, so we were happy to just see what would unfold.

Getting to the farm was our next challenge. I had booked a rental car for our stay in Okinawa, but when I confidently went to pick it up it turned out I had the wrong kind of international driver's license. Mine was a mere translation of my Texas license and not a permit issued by a United Nations recognized body, which is required in Japan and something the police are apparently quite strict about. We had taken a taxi from the airport to Chinen and needed to get from Chinen, in the southeast, to a small village near Naga up north. We spoke to a few taxi drivers and asked them about taking us but they all politely declined. Too far away, it seemed. But we had found a convenient bus app which allowed us to plot a bus path (with a few bus changes) from Chinen to Nago, after which we could take another bus up the coast and ask to be dropped off next to the Tshua primary school. We would then message our hosts who would pick us up at the nearby Lawson Station convenience store. This was not exactly traveling in business class!

All went according to plan and after a long day of multiple bus journeys we met our host, at least the husband half, in the parking lot of the convenience store. He seemed a bit dazed and confused, but I later learned this was just his personality. Maybe a bit socially awkward, but a beautiful soul. He greeted us with a friendly smile and a few words of English, and then proceeded to drive us down the coast, up a steep and winding road, and into the green hills that overlooked the turquoise sea.

When we arrived at the farm, the first thing we noticed was a shed full of cows. *Where were the goats*? Once again, I had just proven to myself how often it is that I see or believe what I want to see or believe. I had wanted this to be a *goat* farm . . . not a *cow* farm! (We did meet the two goats in the profile picture, but that was the extent of the goat population.)

We quickly saw how much more feed a cow consumes than a goat, and that what goes into the mouths of these lactose-producing beasts only partially comes out in the form of milk. Our volunteer

26

services weren't required for milking, but primarily for feeding the cows and clearing away the endless production of poo. On the plus side, we *could* feed the goats a bit of grass once a day if we wanted. But there wasn't a drop of goat milk for consumption.

The Kyuna Dairy Farm was set up by an Okinawan couple who, at least at the farm, simply go by "Otosan" and "Okasan," meaning *father* and *mother* in Japanese. We never learned their real names. Work on the farm was quite physical, in the form of preparing the food and feeding the farm's twenty cows, two goats, two roosters, a dozen chickens, about fifteen rabbits (their numbers changed regularly), and a solitary, rather sad looking, seventeen-year-old boar. We worked a minimum of six hours a day and our first shift started promptly at 6:00 a.m. The routine was somewhat reminiscent of our days as young parents. A newborn's life is pretty much limited to eat, poo, sleep, repeat, and these cows were now our children. We settled into our new routine, which started as the sun was rising, by helping to bring the cows in from the field where they had spent the night. At the end of our day, after they had been milked in the evening, we helped herd them back down the road and into the field again.

When we arrived there were three other volunteers staying at the farm, five working guests being the most the farm could comfortably accommodate. In fact, with the initial mixture of workers, Galina and I had to split up and sleep in separate cabins. I was put in a container-cum-guesthouse with two rickety beds, which I shared with a young, very pleasant, self-proclaimed Italian anarchist. Meanwhile, Galina shared a slightly more "upscale" room (in the fact that its construction was slightly more permanent and that it was next to the toilets and shower) with two French backpackers. We were told that the French girls would be moving on soon and that, once they had moved out, we could move in together.

Our co-workers showed us the ropes, where to store (and wash) our work clothes and boots, and how to start the fire to make hot water for the shower. There was a bunch of scrap wood lying in a pile near the furnace, along with a saw and axe which we had to use to cut wood for the fire. We were about twice the age of our co-workers, but they were all much more experienced than us in how Kyuna operated. In a few days, however, we would become old hands and, when the next batch of volunteers came, we became the trainers.

Mealtimes were an opportunity to get to know our hosts as well as our fellow volunteers. When we arrived at the farm the Italian anarchist, Stefano, had been traveling the world for some time already. He was only twenty-nine, the same age as our oldest child, but we were equals here. He explained to us his philosophy of anarchism, which helped me understand that anarchists have a worse reputation than perhaps they deserve. Stefano does not advocate violence, but he does believe that there should be no governments and that people should, and can under the right circumstances, live in harmony together. "Jesus was an anarchist!" was one of Stefano's quotes when explaining his philosophy.

Stefano was, in my typically judgmental view, simply lost—searching for meaning in life, traveling the world, and hopping from one volunteer job to another.

But were we, twenty years older, really any different?

Galina and I had a bit more money than him, but Stefano helped remind us that we are all searching and, to his credit, he was actually *out* in the world taking action to find his way. As were we.

Stefano decided to move on to a new location about a week after we arrived. We hugged goodbye and wished each other well as he left in search of a commune on Japan's mainland.

He left just as one of several typhoons hit Okinawa during our stay. We hadn't realized typhoon season was upon us, or that Okinawa sits right in the middle of a patch of the Pacific Ocean prone to multiple typhoons during the summer months. Like the Philippines, which often makes news for its propensity to get hit by typhoons, Okinawa endures about ten a year. But Japanese engineering and heavy-duty concrete construction means they are better prepared.

We were hit by a "small" typhoon on the farm, which brought a couple of days of intermittent horizontal rain and a lot of wind. Keeping ourselves dry during the day was a challenge and, because the cows of course had to eat, work still had to be done. However, the up-side was that the rain provided plenty of lubrication for poo removal.

After six days of physical labor, Galina and I had earned a day off. As nice as it was to have some time to not think about which animals needed feeding next, we both felt a small sense of lost purpose as we left the farm for Nago, the nearest city, where we intended to spend the day. Okasan drove us to town and left us at the local supermarket. We had known that bitter gourds (also called bitter melons) were popular in Okinawan cooking, and here we saw the full extent—two aisles in the produce section dedicated to these green, warty, oblong-shaped plants. Technically, bitter gourds are a fruit (since they have seeds) and are similar to a cucumber or chayote, but very bitter. Okinawans chop them up and fry them with egg, tofu, and vegetables. The bitter taste, I'm told, means they are good for the liver and the digestive tract, and I've read more than once that this particular food could well be one of Okinawa's longevity secrets.

The residents eat a lot of them so . . . maybe so.

As the days went by, we started to get into a groove with this "back to basics" lifestyle and work. Galina and I had a shared set of responsibilities each day, and every day we had a clear sense of tangible purpose (to keep the animals alive). We were starting to understand and experience that was something we would need to find for the longer term—something that was part of living a long and fulfilled life.

One morning at breakfast, Okasan told us there were some school children coming to visit the farm and she needed us to clean up the common area space near our bedroom, since they would use it for a butter-making activity. We cleared out our personal things, and about an hour later three buses of school children and their teachers arrived for a visit. They stayed a couple of hours, gawking at us clearing the poo and feeding the cows. I found it somewhat ironic that about seventy-five years earlier, Americans were invading this island with tanks and guns, and now here I was, an American, working as a "hired hand" on a farm. The children spent a bit of time with the farm animals, including the goats and rabbits, and then Okasan led a butter-making class for them. This, we discovered, was something she enjoyed doing, as she saw it as a way to share her life, and nature, with children who grew up in the city.

Moving into our second week on the farm, we started to get notably closer to our hosts, Otosan and Okasan. They were both in their mid-sixties and, similar to Mr. Nagayoshi, were not particularly aware of Okinawa's fame regarding centenarians. They also seemed indifferent to whether they would live to be one hundred, but from what I could see, they will continue to live out their life purpose until the end.

In Japanese there is a specific word which is used to describe one's life purpose: *ikigai*. A number of books have been written about ikigai, and while there is no exact definition of its meaning, some believe the word itself originates from Okinawa. The most common description of ikigai is *one's reason to get out of bed in the morning.* It is described by Dan Buettner in *The Blue Zones* visually using a Venn diagram, where your ikigai is the intersection of four things: what you love, what you are good at, what the world needs, and what you can be paid for.

Okasan acknowledged her own ikigai over dinner one evening when I asked about it.

Six days a week, she leaves the house at 5 a.m. to buy large buckets of tofu, one of the natural supplements to the hay which we fed the cows. After six separate cow feedings, two times clearing the poo, plus other odd jobs, our workday ended around 5 p.m., but both Okasan and Otosan kept working. Okasan would prepare dinner for us all, and Otosan performed the actual cow milking each day, which he usually finished up as the sun was setting and just in time for dinner.

This daily work, along with maintaining the farm, which they love to share with people like us and school groups that come to visit, and selling milk to make a living, is her reason to get out of bed each morning. This was her ikigai and she was very clear about it.

As volunteers, we were provided with three meals a day, although the cows got to eat breakfast before us. We helped bring the cows up from the field each morning and then put out an initial round of feed for them all, as well as all the other animals. Breakfast was eaten together in the farm office located in the barn. Aside from one morning, when Galina and I made Russian pancakes for everyone, we usually ate peanut butter on toast, washed down with coffee. Lunch and dinner were eaten in the main house, family style.

Okasan usually rang the dinner bell around 7:30 each evening. We gathered together, sitting on the floor around the large, typical Japanese-style wooden table. Rice bowls were distributed, followed (almost always) by miso soup. Dinner was usually some kind of "chanpuru," a mixture of tofu, egg and vegetables, occasionally with some meat or even Spam (which became very popular throughout Asia, and especially in Japan, after the war when it was given out by the American military during rebuilding.)

We don't speak Japanese, but Okasan and Otosan knew a bit of English, enough to have a reasonable conversation. We were also fortunate in that throughout most of our stay there was at least one volunteer staying who spoke both Japanese and English, providing some translation help.

By now, dinner was becoming a great time of getting to know one another better. Over dinner one evening, I asked Okasan about another aspect of Okinawan culture that I had read about: the "moai." The moai is a kind of community support group, or mini social network, unique to Okinawa. I wondered how real, or at least how common, such groups really are. It turned out that both Okasan and Otosan were part of a moai. Okasan's group was formed by eight ladies forty years ago, and the same group continues to get together monthly. When their children were small, they gathered in homes so the children could be watched, and the topic of discussions tended to revolve around kids and motherhood. Forty years later, the same moai met at a restaurant (so that no one had to cook) and the talk revolved less around the children and more about who was in the hospital. Interestingly, the moai also provides a financial support system. Members pay monthly "dues" which can then be drawn upon or distributed by the group leader to other members in need, either as a gift or as an interest-free loan.

By this time we had, over a series of dinners, talked about the importance of having a reason to get out of bed each morning (the ikigai), and community support (in part through the moai). I wanted to dig further, however, and understand what values form the basis for how Okasan and Otosan live. I had never given this much thought in my own life, but I was beginning to get a sense that one's life purpose, which will likely include one's profession, needed to be based on a set of core values.

Aside from wanting to understand the values of our hosts, I had been delving into the topic of values with a coaching client just before leaving Singapore. My client was trying to decide what to do with his business; whether to keep pushing forward to grow it, or to sell it, to take the money and run. In our coaching session, I had instinctively asked him to articulate his core values so that he could see if the way he was living and making decisions about his business was aligned with those values. It sounds simple, but often it's not our values which drive what we do. It can be our ego, our fears, our expectations of others and society (the list can go on), which either drive our decisions or get in the way of making a decision. Sitting on the floor around the dinner table with Okasan and Otosan one evening, I had a deep sense that this was not the case with this couple. I asked about their core values and in the lengthy conversation two words stuck out to me in terms of what was driving them: *dreaming* and *sharing*.

"Everyone must have a dream," Okasan said in response to my initial question about values. She always wanted to have something to strive and hope for in life. Otosan then reminded me again about the importance of sharing what we have, and sharing our lives, with others.

During our time on the farm, Okasan and Otosan had not only hosted the hundred or so school children from the city, but two families from Hong Kong had visited the farm to meet the animals and to make butter, as had a group of children with Down syndrome. All this in less than two weeks. Okasan shared about her plans to develop a plot of land into a small sweet potato patch, and a parking area so more people could come to the farm and experience nature by picking sweet potatoes. She and Otosan both wanted to share with as many others as possible the gifts of nature and animals, which they believe have a healing power for people.

Seeing this couple, who were about fifteen years older than us, living and working happily together, and clearly living from a shared set of core values was truly inspirational. Galina and I were going to need to work on defining our values—initially for ourselves—in order to then build a life for our new chapter.

Although we came to the Kyuna Farm as laborers, seeking to learn about Okinawan longevity, we had an experience there that money could not have bought. In fact, this was an experience that cost us virtually nothing. We gave of ourselves for two weeks, helping to care for the cows and other animals, but received so much more in return.

Saying goodbye to Okasan and Otosan at the farm was emotional for all four of us as we had developed an authentic bond with this couple. But our next stop awaited us in the self-proclaimed "longevity village" of Ogimi, just a few miles up the coast.

The Blue Zones features the town of Ogimi by name and any Google search on the village yields numerous photos, videos, and news articles about the place, virtually all mentioning its longevity fame.

Okasan had helped us find a room to sleep in (or rather a floor to sleep on) in the home of an elderly Ogimi couple, Morio and Yetza, who rent out a few of their spare rooms. Morio, who spoke enough English to communicate, was eighty-three, and his wife was in her seventies. They did not get many foreign tourists, mostly Japanese, because they don't list their place on Airbnb. Although we had to share a bathroom with the whole family, we did get a bedroom to ourselves.

Different family members came and went, which was all a bit chaotic at times. We came back one evening to find one of their grown sons asleep in the fetal position on the floor of the dining room. This made me wonder if we were sleeping in the room he normally used. While living in the home, we had the opportunity to speak with Morio about life in this famous town. He himself was a bundle of energy, active in the local bowling league (played outside on the grass) and seemed to be almost constantly fishing. Their house was located right on the coastal highway, so he was constantly walking across the street to check his line.

"You want to go fishing?" Morio asked me one evening.

"Of course!"

He took me fishing later that evening on a nearby bridge. We set up our spot under a lamppost, which I supposed was meant to attract the fish. But after trying both sides of the bridge for a couple of hours with no luck, we returned home late and emptyhanded.

Each day, we borrowed bicycles from our hosts and rode around to visit nearby villages and do some sightseeing. We took a few long rides, during which I would often find myself riding ahead, leaving Galina behind me. My mind drifted on some of these excursions, wondering what we were doing there, what would be next once we had finished our Blue Zone adventure, as well as worrying about what was happening with my business back in Singapore. I can see now that I had a hard time letting go enough to enjoy being there, but at the time it only served to annoy Galina, who was left pedaling in the dust with no communication from me.

Something would need to change in order to make this sustainable.

Riding down the roads throughout Okinawa, both main and side roads, we couldn't help but see cluster after cluster of burial tombs. Made from either reinforced concrete or granite to weather the typhoons, most are the size of small, one-room houses. They dot the landscape like sheep in New Zealand, and we quickly got the feeling that there are just as many tombs on the island as there are houses. The tombs are, in fact, mini houses for the departed and, mathematically speaking, it makes sense that over time there will be more tombs for the dead than houses for the living, if that's not already the case now. Okinawan culture practices a form of ancestor worship whereby the deceased's remains are placed in a tomb, with sufficient space in front of the tomb for family members to come annually to visit, where they will sit, eat, and sing songs. Respect for previous generations is a big deal in Okinawa.

After three nights in Ogimi, and literally just before leaving for our next stop, I asked Morio if he could introduce me to anyone who was one hundred years old.

"Yes, there's one lady nearby and if we go now, we might find her."

I grabbed my phone and, led by Morio, we almost ran to the small road behind the house. It felt like we were on a jungle trek and our guide had just heard there was a three-toed sloth nearby!

We found the lady around the corner. She had just left her house to head out on her bicycle (it was actually a large tricycle, but I think that's forgivable), which she rode every day to the shops. I learned she was also fond of gardening, another well-documented Blue Zone secret. I squatted down to her height for a photo, eager to post it on Instagram—my first encounter with a Blue Zone centenarian. The language barrier handicapped our interaction and Mario's English seemed to get worse when it came to translation, but I did manage to get an answer to my question as to why she'd been able to live to one hundred.

"Ogimi," she said. "It is because I live here."

As simple as that sounds, the environment and culture in Ogimi does really seem to be set up to promote vitality at every age, more than the common notion of joining a gym or choosing the low-calorie salad dressing for lunch. A close community where people stay physically active, eat well and enjoy a pleasant climate - quite a simple formula.

OKINAWA PART II

*"Realize deeply that the present moment is all you
will ever have."*
- Eckhart Tolle

AFTER SAYING GOODBYE TO MORIO and his wife, we moved on to another seaside town, Motobu, famous for hosting one of the largest aquariums in the region. We paid it a visit, along with hundreds of Chinese tourists, then walked back to our home— yet another local guesthouse not available on Airbnb—along the main road and under the hot sun. Just as with the bicycle rides, I found myself walking ahead of Galina, again lost in my own world of thought.

"Why the hell are you walking ahead of me again?" she asked. "It's just like you were doing on the bicycle earlier this week. What are you thinking about?"

The anger and frustration had hit a boiling point, and I didn't have an answer. She unloaded her concerns about how this trip would pan out if I continued to live in a different world from hers and what that would mean for our relationship. "It's not going to work if we go on like this. From now on, we walk side by side and hand in hand."

So was this our new strategy? "Fake it 'til you make it"?

I didn't have any better ideas.

"Okay," I said. "Let's do it."

Aside from the modern aquarium, Motobu is a quaint seaside town with some great seafood restaurants. Soba noodles are the local specialty, and when we went wandering around the old town in search of a bowl each for lunch, we found a gem. *Two* gems, to be exact, in a small restaurant run by *two* ladies, both apparently in their seventies, who work in their tiny kitchen serving up soba noodles for lunch each day. It was so wonderful to see these two ladies working so well together and obviously enjoying what they do, living out their own *ikigais* well into their old age.

With these experiences I started to get the feeling that, as a society, in Okinawa old age doesn't come with any sort of negative spin, as I feel it often does in the West. As an example, take a moment and think about how many "anti-aging" creams and potions there are on the market. Couldn't we instead adopt a mindset of age as being "just a number"? True, we all get older every minute and day of our lives. Eventually our bodies will wear down and we will die. But mentally . . . what is stopping us from living every moment without thinking about age?

After Motobu, we took a short ferry ride to the small island of Ie Jima. It's not far from Motobu, where the only airports are either for emergency or the US military use. As such, it's a relatively quiet place, with a ferry that runs four times a day—unless a typhoon closes them. When that happens the shops sell out of food and the island can be cut off from the Okinawa "mainland" for days.

We had already experienced one typhoon during our stay on the Kyuna Farm, and prior to boarding the ferry we had been warned that another typhoon was approaching. We didn't think much of it as we boarded, despite being told by the ticket lady that the ferry would most likely not be running the next day.

After a short ferry trip, we walked about a hundred meters from Ie Jima's ferry terminal to the guesthouse we had booked for a couple of nights. Our intention had been to simply relax on this small island, enjoy some of its beautiful beaches and climb the solitary ancient volcano in the center of the otherwise very flat terrain. Over a cup of instant coffee, the guesthouse owner, who from the moment we walked in had a very worried expression on his face, explained to us the potential for a "river" to be rushing through their lobby once the typhoon hit. He said they had experienced some intense flooding during the last typhoon, and he noted that of course the island would likely be cut off for who knows how long. The worried owner added that we could stay if we wanted, but he recommended we go back to Motobu that day while the ferries were still running. We somewhat sadly agreed to his suggestion, but he did not want us to leave disappointed and insisted on giving us a personal tour of the island before dropping us back at the ferry terminal. We jumped in his van and he drove us around the island for the best part of two hours. We were able to climb the ancient volcano cone in the center of the island to get a view of the otherwise fritter-flat landscape. The mountain we climbed, we learned, had been hit by so much American ammunition during the war, that its shape visibly changed. Our temporary host drove us around the island a bit more, pointing out the large fenced off section still controlled by the American military, then dropped us off at the ferry terminal. There was no charge for the tour guide services (or penalty for cancelling our reservation), and tipping in Japanese culture is generally considered rude, so I didn't offer him money. It was clear the guy simply wanted to be nice and to make sure we left with positive memories.

But the kindness we experienced on Ie Jima was only a warm-up. After returning to Motobu, we contacted the owner of the house where we had stayed the previous two nights and asked about rebooking with him to wait out the typhoon. He was happy to have us return, but immediately said, "While typhoon is on, guesthouse is free."

As it turned out, the typhoon changed course, which meant it arrived almost a day later than originally forecast. By the time it had come and gone, and we were ready to drive south to Okinawa's main city of Naha, three nights had passed. When it became time to leave, and before I could even offer to pay for our stay, the owner reiterated that our stay was free of charge. Once again, we were amazed at the kindness of this stranger, who took this time of "crisis" to extend a generous and selfless offer to guests, not to mention the fact that he was offering this hospitality to an American.

I can relate to being nice—I'm generally a very nice guy—but these unexpected acts of kindness took me by surprise, leaving a strong impression on me and adding to the fondness and love I felt for the families that had hosted us in Motobu, Ogimi and on the Farm.

***

Coming to Okinawa was our third visit to Japan. Culturally, Okinawa differs in some ways to the mainland of Japan. For example, unlike on the mainland, we didn't notice people bowing when saying hello or goodbye.

Japan has a very closed and unique culture, one that has evolved over the centuries somewhat in isolation. I often refer to Japan as the "Galapagos of humanity." And here I experienced a culture where there is more emphasis on "we" than "me." Maybe this means fewer capitalist-focused entrepreneurs than, for example, in America, but it does seem to result in a culture which fosters community and a willingness to help others.

As we moved on from the north to the south, we spent a few days in Okinawa's capital city, Naha. By this time I had rectified my illegal driver's license status by sending my Texas license to our daughter. She had the proper international license issued and mailed back to me, so we had now been able to rent a car. Ironically, on July 4th, America's Independence Day, we visited "Hacksaw Ridge" where a grueling battle was fought during the US invasion of Okinawa. The heroic acts of Corporal Desmond Doss, a pacifist member of the US Army who refused to use (or even carry) a weapon, were first chronicled in a 2004 documentary, and then made into a movie by Mel Gibson in 2016. Corporal Doss rescued seventy-five of his comrades from the hill, belaying most of them down the face of a sheer cliff. Today, the cliff is still there, and a small sign acknowledges the heroism of Doss. It is otherwise now surrounded by concrete real estate developments, which is pretty much all one sees when looking around Naha. Also visible from Hacksaw Ridge is the expanse of the US military's presence on the island, estimated by locals at taking up around 30% of Okinawa.

***

Not long after we had left Singapore, the reality of being "empty-nesters" on a journey of discovery started to set in. Initially, I told people that I was taking a sabbatical for a year. But it wasn't long into the journey that I realized this was not a sabbatical at all; this was *life*. It was life after children, and we were doing it with a hard press of the 'reset' button.

We realized that, while traveling, we wanted to find a way to engage with local people in the places we would visit, learn from them as much as we could, and contribute something of ourselves in the process. There is a place and time for being a tourist and simply relaxing when visiting a new country or location, but for us this Blue Zone-inspired journey was not a holiday, it was our life. We were not simply taking a break or enjoying a vacation. This was a journey we would *live*.

Becoming WWOOFers and then working on the Kyuna

Dairy Farm had allowed us to accomplish this goal. We wanted to have another similar experience, so while in Naha, we started to look for other WWOOF volunteer opportunities. We were attracted to a listing on the island of Ishigaki, one of Okinawa's southernmost islands. There we reached out to a middle-aged lady who had some horses and had posted that she needed help caring for them from time to time. She rejected us, saying no help was needed, but a few hours later wrote back to say: "My mother is eighty-five and would be happy to have you come and help her." We had previously seen the mother's WWOOF posting, but had skipped over it as it wasn't clear what help the lady wanted, and her reviews were a bit odd. One said "I had to serve tea to her friends when they came over to visit," and another read "She left me alone all day at the house without telling me and left me with nothing to do." But since we had now been invited, and this lady sounded like such a character, we immediately purchased tickets to fly to Ishigaki.

We gave our new host our flight information and she confirmed that she would meet us at the airport. Upon arrival at the small terminal, we met Masako, one of the shortest adults I have ever seen. In fact, she was so short I wondered how she could drive. She managed, but she did have the driver's seat of her small car pulled all the forward and as high as it would go, making her look like she was driving a car at an amusement park.

She drove us to her home, a house built on a few acres in the middle of sugarcane farmland. This was a home, and business, which she had built up since moving to Ishigaki from Naha thirty-five years earlier. She was in the business of plants, we learned, and her main product was henna, which she sells to hair salons. Henna is a natural dye which comes from the leaves of a henna tree (although it is really more like a bush). Masako has rows of henna trees. The natural hair dye is formed by grinding up the leaves and mixing them with lemon juice to form a paste, a solution also used for making henna tattoos.

When we arrived at the home we were greeted by one of her henna leaf buyers, Koji, a hair stylist from Tokyo who specializes in henna. He comes to Ishigaki every year to harvest, and buy, henna from Masako.

We were shown to our room, which was a small addition on the large tool shed-style workshop. The bathroom was adjacent to the kitchen in the main house, a short walk across the parking area that separated the house from the shed. It was the only currently working bathroom in the house, as the other was being renovated (although it seemed the renovation had stopped some time ago). We were getting what we wanted—the chance to truly live with locals and get to know them.

In addition to henna, Masako grew other plants which she sold mostly wholesale to the likes of hotel developers for landscaping. Our first job, assigned almost immediately upon arrival, was to weed a patch of dirt on the main road where a metal sign hung that advertised her business and phone number. After about two hours, our weeding work was done and Masako was happy. It was only proper that the area around her "storefront" didn't appear wild or overgrown.

We had arrived on a Saturday. That evening, over dinner with Koji, Masako announced, "Tomorrow is Sunday. Day off!" She asked Koji to come and get us the next morning and show us around the island.

Koji spent half the day with us before getting us set up with a couple of rented bicycles. This time, I was much better about riding with Galina, staying with her rather than leaving her in the dust. We stopped for a coffee at a seaside restaurant and overheard discussions about a typhoon approaching the island. "Here we go again…" I thought.

The days with Masako started at 8 a.m., when we showed up for coffee and some breakfast, prior to getting our work orders for the day. Masako had usually been up earlier and was always busy doing something. This was a woman who loved to work. In fact, she once said to us, "You must tell me to rest; I love to work so much that I just go and go, but I need to rest sometimes." She had a dry and very witty sense of humor.

During our stay we did some more weeding and general clean-up work, harvested bananas, and planted aloe-vera and a row of cinnamon trees for future generations. However, most of the clean-up work we did was after the typhoon we had heard about over coffee. We had already experienced two "small" typhoons in our previous locations, but this one was big enough to be given a name. In the Western hemisphere, "Maria" would have qualified as a Category-4 hurricane (hurricanes and typhoons are in fact the same kind of storms, they just go by different names in the different hemispheres).

Before Maria hit the island, we had a full day of preparation, which included boarding up windows, dismantling an outdoor tent, and moving or covering up much of the plant inventory.

Houses and infrastructure in Okinawa are built well and, fortunately, the typhoon came and went over about twenty-four hours, causing little serious damage. Galina and I moved into the main house with Masako for the day, as we all felt our little shed might be at risk. The storm was as strong as the few big hurricanes I experienced in Texas. Constant wind, trees flapping around looking like they'd either break in two or fly away, and a constant whirl of small debris in the air.

We stayed inside for about eighteen hours and then emerged to survey the damage. The TV antenna had blown down, as well as one tree. A row of banana trees lay on their sides, but otherwise there was only about a day's work of debris to clean up. While there had been a real sense of concern and preparation as the typhoon approached, life returned to normal pretty much the following day. Masako was incredibly happy that we had been there and was quick the next day at dinner to express her gratitude.

It was a real joy to spend time with Masako and, as the days went by, we got closer to her and learned more about her life. She was born and raised on Okinawa's main island and was a mere ten years old when the war came. She has vivid memories of the American invasion, which impacted her family directly. Her father fought in the war and survived, but her fifteen-year-old brother was a civilian casualty. She didn't speak much about her experiences during that time, but she became visually emotional when she spoke of seeing "a lot of death." She recalled one story of escaping from their village at night, running hand-in-hand with her younger brother through the rice fields to get away from the incoming invasion. After the war, she went on to study English and work as a typist on the American military base, before moving to Ishigaki thirty-five years ago.

Over dinner one evening I asked her how she felt about working for the Americans after they had attacked and conquered her country. "I was never mad," she said. "Past is the past; it's finished." She said that change was necessary and without the war change would not have happened. "My brother died in the war," she reminded us. "But I don't have..." She struggled to find the word in English to complete the sentence. Then, she took her phone, opened Google Translate and began typing. She'd found the word and said, "Hatred... I don't have any hatred."

Masako shared many stories about her long life and family. She has five daughters and one son. The son is the youngest child, and she confirmed our suspicions that, because a son was deemed necessary for social status, there had been no stopping with childbirth until he was born.

She was married to a man who, in her words, loved sake and "other distractions," more than her. He had died ten years earlier and since then, "I've been happy," Masako told me. He racked up debts over the years, which she paid with money from her own work and business in order to protect her name and the names of her children. Despite her struggles, she maintained a dry and witty sense of humor. She refused, however, to visit him at the family burial tomb (or "dead house" as she called it). "He will just ask me for sake . . . and I don't want to give him any!" This was an honest woman.

She did, however, express her gratitude to him for one thing. "He taught me how to die." He had been ill and was, she said, ready to go, so he just stopped eating. Three days later, he was dead.

The key personal learning for me with Masako was about time. In our previous farm experience with the cows, I had quite a sense of responsibility for the animals which required feeding each and every day. In Ishigaki, I initially felt like I'd been demoted when I was assigned a "menial" task like weeding. But when I turned it into an exercise of being present, focusing on each weed picked instead of thinking about how many weeds were left or what time it was, everything changed. I felt content and even joyful at simply being right where I was.

Another difference between Masako's farm and our dairy farm experience was the routine. With animals, especially milking cows, there were specific times things had to be done every day. Plants are not nearly as demanding as animals, so it made the flow of a day very different. I came to Ishigaki ready to get into another work routine, and after a second day of weeding I asked Masako, "So, what's the work plan for tomorrow?" Her reply was simply "Tomorrow is tomorrow." Accomplishing tasks within a given timeframe, or worrying about the future, was simply not a concern to her, at least not at eighty-five years old.

It's almost a paradox to be relaxed and unconcerned about the future while at the same time having ambitions to get things done, such as to make money. But somehow Masako manages to get quite a lot done, makes a living for herself, and still has time for friends and family. Some of her seventeen grandchildren visit her every Sunday morning, and she has a freezer full of popsicles ready for their arrival.

After about a week of work with Masako, including going through the typhoon with her, we took a quick ferry ride over to a neighboring island, Iriomote, for a short break. We were the only non-Japanese tourists on this island. With such beautiful water, awe-inspiring waterfalls, and unspoiled beaches, it was no wonder this island wasn't advertised to foreign tourists. Our simple hotel on the sea had direct views of both the sunset and the sunrise. This was the first time either of us had woken up early enough to not only see the sunrise, but to watch it pop into view over the ocean's horizon. A sunset is easy to watch as it's obvious where the sun is going, but waiting for the fire ball to break up over the horizon, which happens in an instant, is a different kind of anticipation. It took us two days to find the right spot and exact time to catch that magical moment. At the time we were the only people on the beach, whereas the whole hotel seemed to be watching and photographing the sunset each day.

Still the question remained: would we continue to create a life of unique experiences *together,* curated for ourselves, such as this magical sunrise experience, or would we take the tried and true path of least resistance and settle for the sunsets?

***

Throughout our time in Okinawa we had been checking in on the progress of Natasha's pregnancy. She was due at the end of July and we planned to fly to Texas to get there about a week before she gave birth. It was already the second half of July and we really didn't want to miss it, so we used our days off to buy tickets to fly from Ishigaki to Taiwan, where our luggage waited for us in the self-storage unit. From Taiwan we would catch a flight to Houston.

While monitoring Natasha's pregnancy, I also periodically checked in with my mother to see how my dad was doing. He had turned ninety-five while we were in Motobu, just before coming to Ishigaki. He had been healthy throughout his long life and was still in remarkably good health, although his mental state had started to deteriorate over the past two years. There were no signs of Alzheimer's or dementia, just some on and off depression, which had recently become more on than off. Amazingly, the *only* medication he was on was a small antidepressant. Knowing now what I had learned and continued to learn in Okinawa, I realized that he had lost his ikigai. In recent years, it seemed to me his only reason to get up each day was to not die.

The will to survive is embedded in our DNA. It's what keeps people alive in the most horrible of circumstances. This is what now kept him from death. We would go to Houston to see him as well.

Normally, I have a rule to turn my phone off at night before going to bed, ideally at least a couple of hours before sleep. This helps me sleep better and, just as importantly, the phone is off when I wake up. I then make a point of waiting at least an hour in the morning before turning the phone on as I know that the phone will attempt to control me throughout the day. In recent weeks, however, I had made a point of keeping my phone turned on at night in case of a call announcing either an earlier-than-planned birth or an impending death. Subsequently, any time the phone rang, no matter what time of day, my mind rushed to thoughts of life and death. But no phone calls came, and we finished up our stay with Masako over the next few days, accompanying her to the local farmer's market to put some of her plants on consignment there, and just being with her as she went about her life. By now we had become more than "hired hands." For this short period, we shared our lives.

For years Galina and I have had the habit of making a smoothie each morning using whatever greens, berries, and fruits are available from wherever we happen to be. We even traveled with our own mini-blender. In Okinawa, we were able to pick several green plants from the side of the road in addition to those we purchased at the farmers' market. Masako loved this morning tradition and was always eager to see, and taste, what went in the smoothie each day. Our normal morning routine was to have coffee together at 8 a.m., and then start on the day's work, either planting, pruning, or weeding. Then we would take a morning break for our smoothie. Masako would often stop our work by calling out "smoothie time," and then wait for us in the kitchen while we prepared a batch for sharing.

One day she took us on a driving tour around the island, showing us the various edible wild plants that grow on the side of the road. One plant she introduced us to is *chomieso*, which she explained is extremely healthy and grows all over Ishigaki like a weed. It is also known by the locals as "longevity grass." So here we were in Okinawa, one of the Blue Zones, and we'd found an abundantly growing herb which promotes longevity.

Had we found the answer to Okinawa's legendary longevity?

I did a bit of research and, sure enough, this particular plant, which grows predominately on the southernmost islands of Okinawa, including Ishigaki, contains an extremely high concentration of antioxidants. In fact, it seems that its antioxidant content is off the charts. After discovering this, we put chomieso in our smoothies every day. I also learned that the Japanese conglomerate, Shiseido (generally known for their make-up), had set up a facility on a nearby island to harvest chomeiso, and to produce tea and supplements.

After two weeks in Ishigaki with Masako it was time to leave and take one of the few weekly flights out of Ishigaki to Taipei. We purchased a cake in town on our last day and had *Thank You* written on it in icing, and presented it to Masako after dinner. "Wow, this is the first time someone has done this for me," she said, somewhat in shock. While I know she was grateful to us for the help we had provided, including before, during, and after the typhoon, we were also grateful for all she had shared with us. We had, with her, created a Blue Zone experience for ourselves far beyond what we could have ever had simply visiting Okinawa and staying in a hotel.

The mood was solemn as Masako drove us to the airport the next morning. She was sad to see us go and her eyes said it all when we got to the international departure drop-off area. Through slight but noticeable tears building in her eyes, she said goodbye. In true stoic style, so common among tough Okinawans of her generation, she didn't have much to say and it was clear she didn't want to show further emotions, as she stayed in the driver's seat after stopping the car. I walked around to the open window, told her "thank you" one last time, leaned in to give her a hug, and let her know that we would never forget this experience.

We had spent almost two months in Okinawa, visited four different islands and lived with three different families. We had learned about life and values from people in their sixties, seventies, and eighties, plus one centenarian. It was still too early to say how, in practical terms, these experiences would change how we would live, but I had the feeling that we were starting to put our relationship through some kind of pressure or friction.

The coming heat was either going to burn things up or make us stronger.

LIFE AND DEATH

"Life is most delightful when it is on the downward slope, but has not yet reached the abrupt decline."
- Seneca

IN SEASON THREE OF THE HIT Showtime series *Billions*, two of the show's heroes, Axe and Wags, speak about death, after a mutual acquaintance had passed away at the age of thirty-three. The dialogue between the two men standing graveside, goes like this:

"Dying in your thirties is tragic - as is forties. Sympathy dissipates from there."
"Fifties is… 'such a shame.'"
"Sixties is 'too soon.'"
"Seventies 'a good run.'"
"And eighties is 'a life well lived.'"
"Nineties?"
Axe, after a pause, wryly concludes… "That's a fuckin' hell of a ride."

We transited Taipei, picked up the luggage we had left in the storage locker two months earlier, and caught a flight to Houston. We had booked a room on Airbnb—a bedroom—in a typical four-bedroom suburban house near Natasha's apartment. Our host, Olivia, lived in the home with her husband.

The house was a bit more crowded than we had been led to believe by the Airbnb listing. The couple's two grown-up children also lived in the house, including their daughter who was home from college for the summer. She had three small, hyperactive, and very loud dogs caged up in the living room, who exploded into barking every time we entered the house or came downstairs.

This was the first time we had rented a room like this on Airbnb that included living with a family. In the past, when not staying with our own family, we stayed in a hotel or rented an entire house. Clearly our experiences in Okinawa of living with families in close quarters had pushed us out of our comfort zone, and now we were sharing a kitchen, living room, and driveway with four people we didn't know at all. This itself was a new experience made possible by the "shared economy," and our willingness to do something different from what we had done in the past. I also admit that I was happy about paying $30 a night for our one month stay versus more than $100 a night that a hotel or private place would cost.

Had we not had a daughter about to give birth we might have spent a bit more time getting to know the family, as they clearly had an interesting story. Olivia immigrated to the US as a child from the Dominican Republic, and her husband did the same from Honduras. They had met in the US and, over the years, built a life together in Houston.

We had accomplished our goal of getting to Houston in time for the arrival of our third grandchild. Natasha was only a few days from giving birth, so we got our instructions on what to do when the moment came. When she and our son-in-law, Renado, went to the hospital, our job would be to take care of the current children. We needed to stay nearby, but knowing it could be days before our full-time babysitting services were required, we made a routine for ourselves built around a daily CrossFit workout session at a nearby gym (or "box" as they are called in CrossFit lingo).

CrossFit has a reputation for having a cult-like following and being a bit extreme in how it pushes athletes to compete with one another and themselves. We had not experienced it before, but the idea of flipping over tractor tires was pretty exciting to me. The competition was palpable, and each morning the "workout of the day" (WOD) was explained to us by Mike, the owner of the gym, after a warm-up. The WOD was usually a timed group of exercises which included some combination of intense weightlifting, running, rowing machines, or throwing medicine balls either up in the air or to the ground. Knowing that such intensity, combined with the competitive nature of CrossFit, could be a quick path to an injury, I daily had to consciously check my ego at the door. This was a good practice for me as I'm wired to care what other people think of me and often spend unnecessary energy promoting an image of "I've got my shit together," even if I don't. But working out with people who were physically stronger than me, and who pushed themselves more than I felt was necessary for my own level of general fitness, gave me a daily opportunity to let go of comparing myself to others. There were times when all the other men where powerlifting bars with big weights on each end while I did my reps with an empty bar!

So much for looking strong.

Routine is important in life. In our nomadic travel adventures we had begun to realize that we longed for the predictability that came with establishing some kind of daily ritual, wherever we called "home" for more than a few days. So, we quickly adopted CrossFit as our daily "thing" each morning and over the course of the next six weeks only missed one day.

My parents lived about an hour away from where we were staying, but during our initial days in Texas, I took the time to visit at least every other day. My dad was conscious and awake most days when I stopped by, but he always had a nap mid-afternoon.

I did my best to arrive before his naptime so that I could spend some time with him while he was awake. Then I would lie down with him for a few moments before he slipped off to sleep.

One day I sat with him on the side of the bed as he prepared to lie down, and I said that I'd be leaving the house soon to go back to the place we were staying. This news startled him as he had interpreted what I was saying as heading back on the road to visit another Blue Zone. I assured him that I wasn't going away on another trip and that we planned to be in Houston for several weeks to come. He let that sink in for a few seconds and replied "Okay, good. So that means you'll be here for my funeral." I kind of laughed off the shock of these words by saying "Well, that'll be a good trick if you can pull it off."

Somehow, however, I think we both knew he was right.

I went on to assure him that when that day came, it would be a day of celebrating a full and wonderful life.

"Yeah," he sighed, and laid down for his nap.

Only a few more days passed when the call came from Natasha that she and Renado needed to head to the hospital. Baby number three was coming. We were nearby so we drove quickly to take custody of the two grandchildren, feeding them both and getting them to sleep that night. Renado called about 3 a.m. to tell us Natasha had given birth to a boy.

A few days later, along with Natasha, we brought the new baby around to see my dad. He had never been a big fan of babies, and old age tends to magnify dislikes and negative characteristics in a person. By this time, however, Dad didn't seem too bothered, although certainly not too excited or even interested about another great-grandchild being born. He was done.

Natasha came home after one night in the hospital and we moved back in with Olivia and the loud dogs. By now I was playing a daily game of coming downstairs each morning and attempting to make pre-CrossFit coffee without triggering a storm of barks from the yappy dogs. It was a game I never won.

One morning I had a call from my mother. "I think you need to come around today," she said. I was happy to do so but asked why. She went on to explain that Dad had been asking that I come and look at his taxes. This was the first time over the past several years that he had shown any interest at all in his taxes, or about his finances in general. My mother had quietly taken over the family finances about two years ago. This had been a clear sign to us that he was disconnecting, as up until then he had taken the lead role in managing all of that, including preparing tax returns. So I found it interesting that he suddenly wanted to talk taxes.

By the time I came to the house a few hours later I could see that Dad was wanting to speak, and he asked almost immediately that I take him back to his office. I sat with him there and waited to see what it was he wanted to talk about. He began shuffling various papers on his desk, picking things up and looking at them slowly, one at a time. He came to a brokerage account statement which was in one of his well-organized piles of papers. Staring at it for a few moments he handed it to me, or at least attempted to move it in a forward motion in my direction, and asked, "Do you know what this is?"

I took it from him and looked at the paper, noting that the statement showed a balance of cash and securities of something like $30,000, which I explained to him.

"So, you mean to tell me I'm not broke?" he asked.

"No, Daddy, you're not broke," I replied. "You've got this account, plus another savings account and some life insurance policies. Mother will be fine, and I give you my word that I'll do all I can, as well, to take care of her." This seemed to be all he needed to hear that afternoon; not long after, he was fast asleep.

I found that afternoon with my dad to be very poignant. I saw, face to face, the fear of financial failure which had gripped much of his life, including some of my earliest memories of him. Failed business ventures had forced my parents to sell our home west of London when I was seven years old. He then found work back in Houston. Although originally from a small oil-town in north Texas, Houston was his adopted hometown as this was where he had attended university. After graduating from Rice University in 1945, he spent almost two years in the Army, serving in occupied Germany, where he used his electrical engineering degree to support surveillance activities in the search for former SS officers in hiding. He returned to Houston after that experience and lived and worked there for over a decade before moving to Europe. He lived in London for a number of years, living the high life and riding the economic boom of post-war Great Britain. At the age of forty-four he realized it was time to settle down, and he married my mother. I came along two years later.

By all accounts, life was good until the economic turmoil of the early 1970s in England (and globally) hit him hard. He had started his own business several years before, and by 1975 the venture had failed. This left him broke and, even worse, significantly in debt to his financial backers – friends who were then, he found out, no longer so friendly. He chose not to declare bankruptcy, however, and instead agreed to pay off the debt over the next ten years, a timespan which would cover most of my formative years as a growing boy, and a time when I, unfortunately, saw him bearing the weight, and shame, of his perceived financial failure.

And here I was, with him at ninety-five, seeing him wrestle one last time with his past.

I was seven years old when we moved from a large, comfortable house in England to an apartment in a new suburb of Houston. We never missed any meals, but I grew up in what often felt like an environment of scarcity, and felt shame as a child about our family's financial standing versus those of my peers. We lived in an apartment complex for years while most of my friends had houses. I was in high school by the time my parents could finally afford a house. Compounding other financial problems, my dad never seemed to do well with real estate. He and my mother purchased our house at the height of the Texas early 1980s oil and gas boom. The value of the place plummeted within a few years, and they were forced to sell the house at a loss. This created a belief in me that investing in real estate was not a way to make money—in fact, it was a good way to lose money. As a child I was never shown by example how one *could* make money, at least money that would be more than the minimum required to get by. By all accounts my dad had done very well financially before I was born, although I didn't get to see that, and instead interpreted what I experienced over those years into a belief that I did not deserve more money than was necessary to just get by.

My father's money struggles had left me with some deep scars, including my own deep-seated fear of financial failure—fear of ending up like my dad. Since college, that fear led me down an elusive path of chasing financial security, and it continues to be a fear lingering in the back of my mind to this day. I had become aware of this fear only a few years before this poignant time with my dad, and realized how much that fear had dictated significant decisions in my life. But I was grateful, at least at this moment, to be able to empathize with him in his final days on this earth.

As the month of August moved on, Dad was eating less and less and daily becoming notably frailer. He was, by and large, bed-ridden and now spent only a few hours a day sitting in his chair in the living room. His body started to look like photos I'd seen of concentration camp survivors after the war—just skin and bones. Thankfully, he was able to stay at home in his own bed while hospice workers came in most days to check his status and occasionally give him a bath.

After a month at Olivia's house, and after Natasha had given birth, Galina and I moved in with my parents, as we knew Dad's days were numbered. This allowed us to be in the house and host a few final visitors, including Natasha and her family whom we called to suggest they come to say a final goodbye. By now Dad no longer asked for food and we had to dab a sponge in his mouth for hydration. One afternoon, I asked him if he wanted an ice cream to which he perked up with a hearty, "Yes, please!" So, together on his bed, we shared a vanilla ice cream . . . the last bit of food he would ever eat.

I spent time each day lying on the bed next to him, as I'd done over the preceding weeks. "I'm not seeing very well now," he said, the day after our ice cream. "What's happening? I don't understand what's going on."

"Your body's just shutting down. It's okay," I said.

"Goodbye," he whispered in my ear before falling asleep.

Those were his last words to me.

The next day he managed to exchange a few final words with his pastor. "Please take care of Rosemary," he said. The pastor assured him that he'd do all he could to make sure his wife would be taken care of, then said a final prayer over him. My father never spoke again.

The following day at about 3 a.m., my mother knocked on the door of the bedroom where Galina and I were sleeping. She entered, shaking slightly and through soft tears said, "I think he's gone."

I got up quickly and went to his room. He was lying peacefully in bed, his breaths having finally come to an end. He had passed away in his sleep while lying next to his wife of over fifty years.

What better way for anyone to go? For me, being there for this life event was such an honor, it felt like a perfectly ordained end to a chapter.

A few weeks prior, the hospice worker had given us the phone number to the twenty-four-hour "corpse collection hotline." I dialed the number and informed the man who answered of the passing.

"I'm sorry for your loss," he said, which became the first of many occasions I would hear those words in the coming days. "I'll be over as soon as I can…"

Galina, my mother, and I made a pot of tea, exchanged a few hugs, and waited. It was still dark outside when I opened the door to a big-haired, elderly gentlemen dressed in a dark suit and tie. "I'm sorry for your loss," he said once again as I welcomed him into the house.

He introduced himself as Ben, a long-time friend of the funeral home, and the man usually charged with night duty for the area. After the short introduction, and another, "I'm sorry for your loss" for my mother, Ben asked, "Could you show me the body please so I can see how to best get him out?"

The bedroom was just down the hallway with only one sharp, right turn, and after a brief survey of the situation Ben returned from his van with a gurney, complete with restraining straps. I accompanied him to the room and, since he was alone and looked like he might need some help, I offered my assistance in getting Dad off the bed and onto the stretcher. He graciously accepted, saying, "I usually don't get that offer."

Once situated and before covering his head, Ben offered my mother a chance to say goodbye, at least for that day. "He looks so peaceful," she said, then Ben rolled him down the hall, around the corner, and out the front door for the last time.

Just before we headed out, I remembered my dad joking, "The

last time I leave this house will be feet first!" which was a clear statement of his intent and will to die at home and not in a hospital. He got his wish and, just to be sure it was honored completely, I told Ben we needed to turn him around so that his feet did indeed go out first. My mother and Galina laughed hysterically—a nice gift that Dad had been able to give us to lighten the mood of an otherwise somber occasion (and, incidentally, the one day we would miss our daily CrossFit workout).

Dad had always talked about death in a light-hearted manner and was never in denial about the fact that he would die one day. He talked about being "planted" somewhere nice, maybe on the side of the highway so it would be easy to get to, or wave from. I remember him teaching me a poem when I was young, the first time I saw the very distinct shape of an American hearse. It's a poem of unknown origin with varying lyrics, including a longer version available on YouTube, but my dad's version, which I still find myself singing whenever I see a hearse, went like this:

Did you ever think when the hearse rolls by
Someday you're going to die
They'll wrap you up in a woolen shirt
And cover you over with gravel and dirt
The worms crawl in, the worms crawl out
The worms play pinocle over your snout
You're gonna rot without a doubt.

I found myself singing that song again as Dad left his home of almost twenty-five years for the last time. He was always one for a good laugh and, as my mother said that early morning, "He got the last laugh on the way out the door."

I had not expected that helping to usher someone from this life to the next could actually be joyous. At some level I had dreaded the thought of being physically present with someone, especially a loved one, in their final days, much less being present for their death. The thought of having to help someone deal with their physical limitations, in addition to being with them as they looked death in the eye, in the past would have caused a fair amount of anxiety. But, as with many things we fear in life, once I "just did it," any anxiety slipped away, and I was able to calmly and confidently accompany him on his final walk home.

***

My father's service in the US Army from 1944 to 1946 qualified him for a military funeral. This included a trumpeter playing "Taps" and retired servicemen firing a few rounds from their guns in his honor. The graveside funeral was the first I had attended, and watching the coffin as it was lowered into the ground brought death's stark reality home. We all die and, for the most part, end up as ashes scattered or lowered into a hole in the ground.

My dad was blessed with ninety-five years to make the most of his life and for the most part I believe he did. He had experienced life from the Great Depression to World War II and on to the boom times in Europe and the United States which followed. He was married to only one woman, for over fifty years, had two children, and many friends.

I found it hard to be too sad about his passing, and felt more anger than sadness—anger that I had never *really* known the man.

I believe his personal ambitions and fear of financial failure had kept him closed off emotionally, at least to me, which got in the way of me having a close relationship with him. I also know that this was not uncommon for men of his generation. We never fought or had harsh words, which perhaps in itself was a sign that something was a bit off. Our relationship was certainly respectful, but not deep. He never probed me on how I was *really* doing in key areas of my life, and for years I felt that he somehow lived vicariously through me, to the extent that any failure or discontent in my life would be a negative for him. I felt this led to a certain amount of pressure to be seen by him as being "successful," so that he could feel good about himself. His passing made this clearer, and I felt angry at myself for having allowed myself to live under that pressure. Yet there was also a kind of relief that this dynamic was now over. Gone.

Fortunately, I had dealt with the larger issue around my father's financial failures—and my own hurt and anger around that—about eighteen months before his passing. This big shift came through writing his eulogy, which I did, in part, so I would have it ready for when the time came. I also knew it would be a cathartic process.

I started by taking the obituary that Dad had drafted for us to publish in the local newspaper after he passed. He had typed it up with the introduction: "Hugh A. Saye passed away on _____," leaving the blank for us to fill in when the time came. He then went on to give an overview of his life and all the places he'd lived and worked. Although his hobbies and family received mentions in the text, the vast majority of what he wrote was about his career and education.

I don't believe it is unusual, especially for men, to want to be remembered for their esteemed careers, but it still struck me as a bit odd since I had never really seen my dad as having been vastly successful in business. For as long as I could remember, he had struggled to get ahead financially. But by putting myself in his shoes, when he was in the middle of his life and at about the same age as me now, I was able to empathize with the man I otherwise didn't really know. I was able to see, and feel, how the financial "failure" he experienced shortly after getting married and having two children, would have hit him hard. I don't believe he ever truly got over that loss, and he spent a lot of energy in the years that followed trying to make amends and prove to himself that he wasn't a failure. Even though it was now too late to speak to him about this, I still found some peace in letting go of the anger and shame I felt about what I had perceived as him letting me down financially.

I began the eulogy that I would deliver at his remembrance service with the question, "How does a man want to be remembered?" The rest went as follows:

I believe this is a question most people don't necessarily contemplate during the course of their lifetime. It may come at the end of life, at a time when there's little opportunity to change and be remembered in the way he wants. I can't say that I ever asked my dad this question specifically, but judging from the obituary he wrote for himself, it was clear that his career accomplishments and life adventures were the things important to him. However, from the feedback I've had recently and over the years, the reality is that he is being remembered for his character and not his accomplishments. Or in other words, who he was, not what he did.

I know that his life was much more than his career and the vast library of stories from his days as a boy growing up in the wilds of north Texas, his years of studying electrical engineering at Rice, time spent in occupied Germany after the war and then during the post-war glory days working in Europe.

Ninety-five years is a lot of history and my dad saw tremendous change in the world over the course of his life. He had memories as a boy of an old guy named "Dick," a former slave who lived in his town. Dick was, of course, by then a free man but this was an era where Blacks were still legally treated as a lower class with less rights. Fast forward through most of his lifetime and a few years ago my dad was able to openly and authentically welcome Renado into our family, also a descendant of slaves. This was an example of one of his greatest traits—loving people as people, irrespective of race, class, or whatever. As a man brought up in "the good old days," he certainly had his views on things like gay marriage and gun control, but I know for a fact that if it came to a personal level he would be open, non-judgmental, and loving to anyone he met—gay, straight, and even the democrat or two who strayed into his life. His ability to make people feel special and loved was one of his most endearing characteristics.

Integrity is when one's outer actions are consistent and in harmony with one's inner moral and ethical beliefs. My father was a man of high moral conviction stemming, which I have to believe, from his deep and sincere Christian faith. He was an honest man. A good man.

It was his faith and integrity which stand out to me as symbols of a period of time he may have wanted to forget but which heavily influenced my life. The catalyst for bringing his family back to America in 1976 was the economic crisis which hit England, and thus our family, in the mid-1970s. I was barely, if at all, conscious of what was going on, but I know this took a toll on him, a newly married successful businessman who had, by all accounts, up until then an exciting, fulfilling, and profitable career in post-war boom times.

One of his lesser-told stories was how, at the height of financial stress, while sitting in the bedroom with my mother, he held his Bible and, looking her in the eye said, "Are we going to believe what is in here or shall I throw it out the window right now?" He was serious. That was a pivotal moment in his life, a moment when he chose to hang on to his faith and stay true to his family and obligations.

An opportunity to move to America and start a new chapter in life came within days and a new life began for us all. Even though I was only seven at the time, the character he showed, as he led us to rebuild our lives in Texas and honorably work his way out of debt while remaining faithful to God, his wife, and his children, left an indelible mark on my soul. While not even knowing it at the time, through those trials and tribulations and in the years to come, he passed the flame of faith, honesty, and integrity to me and to many others who came into his life.

Today we say goodbye and give thanks for a life well-lived. A long life full of fun and adventure, creating a family and a legacy of faith, love, and integrity.

My father always said there would be surprises in Heaven and I'm sure he is delighting in them now. To me, words from the Gospel of Matthew in the parable of the talents come to mind, and I don't doubt this is what he heard when he passed from this life to the next: "Well done, good and faithful servant. You have been faithful with a few things . . . Come and share your Master's happiness."

Writing this eulogy while my dad was still alive helped me to see, through his eyes, how much pain and turmoil he must have experienced when I was young and he had suffered his financial losses. I was able to look at him through new eyes—not with pity but with compassion. Until then, I had focused, to varying degrees, on how his losses had impacted *me* and deprived *me* of certain material benefits growing up. And while that was still true, once I took my eyes off myself, the financial set-backs took on a new light and I was able to let go of the hurt, anger and victim story which I had been carrying around. Through that, I did feel closer to him, even if I still didn't truly know the real Hugh Saye.

It's also not fair for me to blame my dad for our less-than-perfect relationship. I want to be clear that I mean no disrespect to him with my critique of the dynamics at work between us. It became clear to me at his funeral, and even in the time since, that my dad touched the lives of many and is fondly remembered as an encourager and giver of wisdom. Father-son relationships can be tricky for reasons I don't fully understand. Family patterns tend to repeat themselves based on examples set by previous generations. So one of the lessons for me from my dad's death is to let my own children, and grandchildren, *really* get to know the authentic me – warts and all.

Although he didn't live in a Blue Zone, Dad's life was characterized by several Blue Zone commonalities, the biggest related to how he ate and treated food. He almost always ate small—or at least reasonable—portion sizes. He was far from being a vegan or vegetarian, but I never saw him overeat or use food (or alcohol) as a means of dealing with stress. Even during a Thanksgiving meal, times when I would tend to eat as much as humanly possible, he would not overindulge. He was never overweight. He didn't smoke, he drank alcohol in moderation, and worked out regularly, even before working out was in fashion. He bought a stationary bicycle for cardio exercise in 1980—years before things like that became mainstream. He maintained a healthy social network throughout his life—largely centered around church—and he also played his clarinet in various bands almost his entire life. He ticked many of the key Blue Zone boxes, and this, combined with what must be good genes, helped him live a long life.

Being present with my father and witnessing his death was, for me, in a way as joyous a life event as the birth of our third grandchild three weeks earlier. His was not a life cut short, nor was it a death that was difficult to watch as he didn't appear to be in much pain or struggle as he faded away in those final days. I don't envy anyone having to watch someone die at a young age or someone dying under strained physical or emotional conditions, but who can complain about death at ninety-five? He'd really had "a hell of a ride!"

I was given the gift of seeing death, and the actual passing, as a very normal and natural part of life—something not to be feared, much less ignored. I'm grateful for this parting gift from my father and his timing could not have been any better.

I am exactly fifty years old as I write these words, halfway to one hundred. I've already experienced a lot in these years, and I'm looking forward to another full and active fifty. I was inspired by my dad's passing to live as though I still have lots to do and lots to contribute going forward. The best is yet to come.

Top: An emotional good-bye to Otosan and Okasan at their farm near Ogimi, Okinawa.
Middle: Hard work at the Kyuna Farm made me feel happy and fulfilled.
Bottom: We weathered a typhoon with Masako on the island of Ishigaki, Okinawa.

In Costa Rica family values were on display in the kitchen with Hermida *(above)* and on the porch with Alfonso *(below)*.

Posing with Chinese tourists under the Northern Lights near
Murmansk, Russia (photo credit: Alexander Stepanenko).

The official certificate on the
wall of the "Longevity Bar"
in Perdasdefogu, Sardinia
where I was told "hard work"
was the secret to a long life.

Me with the widow Maria in Meana Sardo – proof of no old age homes in Sardinia.

Searching for the Holy Grail in Jordan – I was getting closer.

For Galina, life in Ikaria was reminiscent of her childhood in Siberia - simple, and very "green" living.

George Karimalis holds court over dinner with family and guests at his and wife Eleni's farm and winery in Ikaria.

COSTA RICA

*"Too many people, when they get old, think that they have
to live by the calendar."*
- Senator John Glenn

MY FATHER TIMED HIS DEATH PERFECTLY. A few months beforehand, Galina and I had planned to begin two weeks of Spanish language lessons in Nicoya, Costa Rica, starting mid-September. By the first week of September—Labor Day weekend in the US—it had been about two weeks since I had escorted Dad out of the house "feet first," and all of the family was starting to feel ready to get on with life again.

"Getting on with life" meant different things to each of us. My sister had returned to England where she had her part-time job and two children to finish raising. Our daughter was more than busy with her newborn and getting ready to move into the new house they were building north of Houston. Nicholas had started his second year of university in Spain, while Marcus was keeping himself busy in Singapore during a gap year, before starting university in London. Even my mother was feeling positive about her newfound freedom to travel and was contemplating a move to a smaller place.

For us, getting back to life meant continuing our Blue Zone travels and hoping that it would lead to us figuring out what would be next. In our hearts, we knew that this Blue Zone adventure, as interesting and fun as it was, was something we had come up with to delay the inevitable. We were floating between stages in life—homeless and aimless in a way, and at times, feeling a distinct lack of purpose as a couple now that our children were grown up. But at least by having the Blue Zones to visit we had a target to aim for. For now, at least, we were moving and this gave us hope that we would figure things out at some point.

We had given ourselves roughly a year to visit the Blue Zones, which we intended to intersperse with some other travels, but by the following summer we would need to have a plan for somewhere to live. Given that I have a British passport, and in time Galina could presumably get one if we lived there long enough, our plan was to move to the UK after the Blue Zones and begin our new phase of life there. But exactly *where,* and what to build our lives around remained unknown. We knew it would seem our Blue Zone travels would be over in the blink of an eye, and it would be wise to start planning now for what would come next.

Galina, always resourceful when it comes to problem-solving, set out to at least answer the first part of our dilemma—where to go next? She found the answer; we would spend the following summer traveling around the UK, experiencing life in different parts of the country. This would give us a sense of where we wanted to live once our Blue Zone experience had ended.

And how were we going to do this traveling? As pet-sitters!

Galina had discovered a house and pet-sitting service, TrustedHouseSitters.com, which matches pet-lovers who have a desire to travel with pet-owners who want to leave their pets at home while they go away, perhaps for a holiday or work. Owners and sitters each create online profiles, complete with pictures of dogs, cats and other pets, and owners post the dates they need covered. Sitters are encouraged to submit police reports to verify their reliability and trustworthiness. Owners choose from sitters that have applied for their particular sit, usually after on-line interviews, and dates and logistics are then confirmed. As a sitter completes more sits, their credibility improves, thus elevating the chances of being chosen for subsequent sitting assignments.

In order to pull off this plan, and with a new TrustedHouseSitter profile, we had to quickly position ourselves as sincere pet-lovers. Never mind that our experience with family pets was somewhat tenuous...

Our sorted history began with a dog, a beautiful chocolate Labrador, whom we bought for our daughter Natasha when living in Kazakhstan. We lived in a house, although Toby lived outside, and she and Natasha had a great friendship. But less than a year later I was unexpectedly asked to relocate to Moscow for work. Galina and I couldn't get our heads around living in an apartment with a dog like Toby, so we found her a new home in Kazakhstan. Taking Natasha and Toby to her new home and saying a final goodbye was not easy. In hindsight we may have been wrong to leave Toby behind as it was emotionally traumatic for Natasha. But that's just one entry on our list of parenting mistakes.

Toby was fine, however, and went on to live a long and happy life. Not so true for future pets that would come into our lives. A few years later and while living in Moscow, we encouraged Natasha with a few smaller pets. A rabbit, who lived on our tenth-floor balcony, was the first to come . . . and then go . . . in the middle of winter. He managed to squeeze through a drainpipe on the balcony and fell to his death on the atrium roof below. Natasha was forced to have an awkward conversation with the building's security guard to retrieve the stiff, and very frozen, body from the snowy roof.

Next came two hamsters, both of whom were eager to escape from their cage nearly every night. I think they only lasted a few weeks before one slipped into the toilet and drowned, while the other escaped and was never found.

For our TrustedHouseSitter profile we highlighted our respective pet experiences *before* starting a family together. Pets in Siberia weren't quite afforded the same status in families as they are in modern America. Cats were owned for the primary purpose of rodent control, and a dog's main purpose was to make noise when strangers or neighbors came around. They ate leftovers and were never let in the house, even when it was -40 degrees outside. Pet ownership, like most things in Siberia, was about what was practical for survival, and not so much about having a pet as a family friend, much less as a fashion accessory. But that didn't stop us from highlighting in our profile the truth that Galina was "brought up with lots of animals in the household, including dogs and cats." She'd also had a family cow, plus pigs, all of whom ended up on the dinner table, although we left that bit of information off the profile.

As a child I had a dog who was a close companion in the classic sense of a childhood pet, so we at least had this bit of history for the profile. My childhood history with cats, however, was more of a struggle. My parents were not cat lovers, it may not be a stretch to even call them cat *haters*, and this shaped my view of the feline world from a young age. I grew up hearing stories from my dad about how he shot cats as a child and, when an unwanted litter was born in their neighborhood, it was usual practice to put the kittens in a burlap sack, throw in a brick or two, and toss the bag in a pond.

I was never encouraged to kill cats, but I did, as a teenager, accompany my dad on a "cat relocation mission." We had been annoyed by one particular cat that kept coming around our house to visit. She taunted my dog and made noise at night. Rather than find a burlap sack, my dad caught the cat in a plastic trash can and we drove it to a remote location a few miles away and released it "into the wild." We never saw it again.

In college, I discovered that I had an allergy to cats, which further cemented my view that they were to be kept out of my life. But many of the advertised pet sits on TrustedHouseSitters included cats, so I felt it was time to reconsider my point of view, even if it involved allergy medicine.

Our TrustedHouseSitter profile also required us to have some photos of us with pets, and the more the better to show our love for the animal kingdom. We started with the yappy dogs at Olivia's place and staged a great shot of us sitting with them, all smiles, on the couch. We also asked a few random people on the street if we could pose for a photo with their dogs. Our profile was starting to come together.

Now it was time to start applying for pet sits. Without a track record as sitters on the site, we knew we would need to put our best foot forward to get our first gig. We applied for a few sits in the Houston area and, in each application, I did my best to make a personal connection with the pet owner. If they had children, I wrote a bit about our own children. I played up the fact that we were empty-nesters looking to share our love with some pets as a kind of surrogate for our own children. And there was truth in this. Being responsible for someone on a daily basis, even an animal, gives a sense of purpose. My mom had spent the past two years caring for my father and, in spite of the burden it was at times, it had become her purpose—her *ikigai* for a season. She was already discovering that she needed to find new connections and new reasons to get out of bed each day, and I began to see how we also needed to do the same in this new phase of our lives.

Once we finished our Blue Zone travels, we could use this service to stay in different homes around the UK and take care of some pets. Purpose! We finished up our TrustedHouseSitter online profile and made our initial applications just as we purchased our tickets to Costa Rica. We would continue to work on our post-Blue Zone plans while traveling, but for now it was time to get back to the task at hand.

***

The Blue Zone of Costa Rica is located on the Nicoya Peninsula, an area in the northwest of the country on the Pacific Ocean. We purposely chose to begin our Costa Rican adventures in the town of Nicoya, which is almost right in the middle of the Nicoya Peninsula. The Gulf of Nicoya to the east separates much of the peninsula from Costa Rica's mainland. This is the area of Costa Rica that Dan Buettner and his National Geographic team identified in their research as being one of the five "official" Blue Zones. Its relative isolation from the rest of the country has likely played a role in longevity there because in centuries past, the geography kept its gene pool relatively isolated. The strongest survived in isolation, and passed their strong genes to subsequent generations.

We flew from Houston to Liberia, a city in the north of the country, not far from the border with Nicaragua. From Liberia, we had to travel a few hours by bus to get to Nicoya. Of all the foreigners on the United Airlines flight, we were the *only* passengers who made their way to the airport bus stop, and we were the only foreigners on the three-hour, $3 bus ride south to Nicoya. But with about six weeks planned for our time in Costa Rica, and nothing for the first two weeks except Spanish lessons, we weren't in a hurry.

We had booked our first night on Airbnb, in the home of Jaime and Olga, a husband and wife with a spare bedroom. Here we quickly found out that, contrary to our experience in Okinawa, the local population knew about their status as a Blue Zone. Serendipitously, in the past, Jaime had served on the board of trustees at the local old folks' home, and knew a thing or two about aging in Nicoya. We explained our interest in Nicoya as a Blue Zone and he encouraged us to visit the home during our stay.

Somehow, over coffee and corn tortillas, the subject turned to sex. We had read in *The Blue Zones* that, despite being quite religious in general, Nicoyans have fairly liberal attitudes towards sex and fidelity, an attitude that translated into staying sexually active late in life. Jaime confirmed that there was quite a high rate of sexual activity that takes place behind closed doors in the old folks' home. He proceeded to tell us a story of one active gentleman who, having agreed with a female neighbor to a tryst together, got "stuck." One of the pair called for help and a small team of nurses had to come to their rescue.

According to Buettner, stomach cancer rates in the Nicoya Peninsula are 24% lower than the rest of Costa Rica, a significant statistic. That may have more to do with what Nicoyans put in their stomachs than their genes.

Buettner's chapter covering Costa Rica in *The Blue Zones* starts with the lead-in: Tortillas and beans, hard work, and something in the water?

As we had experienced in Okinawa, the book painted a vivid and accurate picture of what we were about to experience in Costa Rica. In Nicoya, we found ourselves eating tortillas every day at some point or another, all made from maize (corn). Both red and black beans were also often included for breakfast and dinner. Meat—beef and pork—was fairly common, eaten in soups and cooked inside tamales, although the quantity of meat was relatively low. Most of the protein eaten in Nicoya comes from beans.

Regarding the water, according to the Blue Zones website, "Nicoyan water has the country's highest calcium content, perhaps explaining the lower rates of heart disease, as well as stronger bones and fewer hip fractures."[ii] Drinking hard water is therefore recommended for improving longevity. Maybe it helps with libido as well.

Nicoya is by no means a tourist town and in the two weeks we spent there we saw or heard less than ten foreigners. That's unusual for a visit to Costa Rica as the country hosts well over two million tourists a year, in addition to the many foreigners who have moved there in search of *pura vida* ("pure life"), Costa Rica's catchphrase and brand. The town of Nicoya had no hotels aimed at tourists and the only global brands we saw on the streets were Coca-Cola and Pepsi. Pretty much everything else was local, aside from the recently built KFC on the edge of town.

As planned, we took Spanish lessons the first two weeks. This would not only be practical in terms of improving our language skills (Galina was basically fluent, while my level was simply basic), but it would allow us to have some structure, meet locals and formulate a plan for what would come next.

We had no idea where we would go after these initial two weeks, but we knew if we set an intention to experience real life and make some real human connections, and if we stayed open to what would come, we would be rewarded.

We signed up for four hours of private lessons per day, and walked to and from class each morning. On arrival, we had a short group chat, mostly in Spanish, about what was happening in the world, and then broke off into our private lessons. The mild-mannered Diego was my teacher and although we used a textbook as a guide, we mostly just spoke. He asked questions with inspiration from the text and then I'd try as best I could to piece together a passable answer. After a break for lunch we'd continue for another two hours in the afternoon.

In addition to the in-class work, the school organized some sort of excursion to the town on most days. One day we hiked to the top of the nearby hill overlooking the city, another morning we visited the local market, which was always a good place to practice vocabulary and numbers. Sweet potatoes, like in Okinawa, were widely on display, as was yucca and another local staple, the chayote, a pear-shaped gourd and technically a fruit, eaten with many Costa Rican meals. Tasteless would be a good way to describe the chayote, but it does the job of getting food into the stomach and, as with sweet potatoes and yucca, since it's not a starch it doesn't turn into sugar. Historically, the local diet would be low on sugar, although there are plenty of other sources of sugar in the modern Costa Rican diet, with Pepsi and Coca-Cola high on the list.

The language school had organized a homestay for us for two weeks. After our first night with Jaime and Olga and learning about old-age promiscuity, we moved in to the guesthouse of Maria and Jose. Our simple room, and shower with toilet, were located along the back fence of their small garden and behind the main house, a simple and small three-bedroom concrete structure. Maria's ninety-five-year-old mother, as well as her unemployed, alcoholic brother, Diego, also lived in the main house. They all seemed to just about tolerate each other.

Maria made us breakfast each morning - tortillas, eggs, and usually some sort of meat or beans, which we ate in the main house by ourselves. Each evening we ate dinner together with Maria and Jose, and although they did not speak a word of English, we were able to practice our Spanish over the meals. Galina did most of the talking, but I followed along and clumsily participated where I could.

Diego was, conspicuously, never invited to have dinner with us, a dynamic I couldn't quite figure out, but I asked him one evening after dinner to take me to "bingo night," which was being held at the community center across the street. This was to be a true immersion into the language and local culture—a local affair hosted by a local church, presumably as an outreach as well as for fellowship. We arrived after a few games had already been played and all eyes focused on me—the sole gringo at the event—when I walked in with Diego. I quickly got the feeling that he was known to the community and, although tolerated at an outreach event like this, he caught a stern eye from one of the ladies when she saw him discreetly pulling out his flask of hooch to sneak a drink. There was free food, tortillas with pork and Pepsi for all, in exchange for buying bingo cards to play each round. I could only manage two cards per game, and it was good practice for Spanish numbers. We used kernels of corn to cover up the numbers as they were called out. Community and religion, two important Blue Zone longevity factors, were both on display for me that evening.

Our language school also managed to organize a visit to the town's elderly care home, the same one Jaime told us about on our first night in Costa Rica. We joined the tail end of a Bible study class, where the active participants were busy coloring pictures of Jesus and Mother Mary, just like in a first grade Sunday school. A few couldn't be bothered to color, but I tried my hand at the artwork just to break the ice. Galina managed to get fairly deep into conversation with a hundred-year-old man. (Given what we'd heard about the place, I didn't want Galina too far out of my sight, but once I saw the relatively low speed at which the guys moved, I realized she was safe!) He had already outlived some of his children and credited his longevity to consistent movement.

Costa Rica is not a typical emerging market and, although not as developed as Europe or the US, I was surprised to see that most families own cars. This contrasts with the proliferation of motorcycles you see in most of Asia's emerging market countries. Also, the public health system in Costa Rica is one of the best, maybe even *the* best, in Central America. From the looks of how the police show up on the streets (well equipped) and how they interact in a friendly manner with the population, corruption doesn't seem to be rampant. Generally speaking, people seem to live good lives in Costa Rica.

Historically, people of the Nicoya peninsula were farmers, which meant a lot of hard work and exercise, including walking between villages, often traversing large hills back and forth. One weekend, Maria and Jose drove us to the town of Quebrada Honda, where she introduced us to her ninety-four-year-old uncle, Rafael. He was so poor as a youth, he had to quit school in the 6th grade and go to work in the fields with a machete. He is still going strong and lives on his own in the village, in a small house just across the street from his village church. Very convenient given he is a deeply religious man. Since gaining notoriety as a Blue Zone, Rafael had been interviewed more than once by visiting international TV crews creating documentaries on longevity.

Because Galina and I weren't working on a farm in Nicoya, we made daily exercise part of our routine. We generally travel with a basic set of workout equipment like yoga mats, blocks, stretch bands, and even a set of gymnastic rings. But here in Nicoya, we decided joining a local gym would be a great way to meet local people and provide a good excuse to get out of the house. There was only one gym in town, aptly called "Jose & Jose," named after the unlikely couple who established the place. The first floor was full of exceptionally large biceps getting bigger on all sorts of machines and free weights, whereas the second floor was for a daily one-hour group class, a high-intensity interval training (HIIT) work-out led by Jose #1. He blew his whistle at us throughout the workout and did his best to encourage us. "*Con ganas, chicos, con ganas!*" (With passion, guys, with passion!"), he'd scream while we did burpees, lifted weights, and so on. As with bingo-night, we were consistently the only gringos working out at the gym.

Planning our next steps, both for Costa Rica and beyond, we logged on to TrustedHousedSitters and WorkAway, the volunteer worksite we discovered while in Okinawa.

We were also starting to plan for the following summer in England and began applying for pet-sitting jobs there. A few pet owners, who were going away on holiday during that time and wanted someone responsible to stay in their homes, made contact and we had some Skype interviews with families in the UK. We also applied for a "sit" in Houston for the end of October, the timing of which would coincide with our planned return from Costa Rica, and help us build up a track record of sitting.

We had a small celebration when our first application was accepted, confirmed for the end of October to take care of an eleven-year-old dog named Hope, in Houston. Not only would this be our first "credential" as house and pet-sitters, it also gave us a date by when we needed to leave Costa Rica, in about five weeks' time. Shortly after Hope's confirmation, one of the applications we had made in the UK was also confirmed. We would be looking after a German shepherd there for two weeks the following August, almost a year away. (I admit that we were impressed that there were people in the world who, unlike us, managed to plan so far in advance.)

As to our more immediate plans in Costa Rica, we focused on WorkAway, and found a few different opportunities to help people out in exchange for room and board. Babysitting and teaching English to a child was one, but we felt slightly over-qualified for that job. Another, which stood out to us, was an American couple, Wendy and Erich, with a home and large property previously used as a retreat center. They needed help with some gardening and odd jobs around the house, and appeared to be warm and friendly, so we applied letting them know we could be there within a few days and stay for up to two weeks. We briefly explained what we were doing in Costa Rica and where we were in our life journey. My email to Wendy helped create a connection and we were invited to come and do some work.

Our intention, on these Blue Zone travels, was to live as "locally" as possible, in order to get a glimpse of regional life and, more importantly, to connect authentically with the people. It's one thing to visit a place and to meet locals for a meal or over coffee, yet a completely different experience to live in their homes for days, or even weeks, at a time. In Okinawa, we spent over half our time living in the homes of, and even working alongside Okinawans. Through that, we gained invaluable insights to how they live, their personal values, and more. Our aim in Costa Rica was to do the same.

By this time we had spent two weeks living with a family in Nicoya while we attended our daily Spanish classes and had begun to feel like members of the family. But now we would leave the Nicoya Peninsula and head to the Costa Rican mainland. Wendy and Erich's three-acre estate was located in the mountains above San Jose, the nation's capital.

On our last day of Spanish classes, we rented a small jeep that we ended up keeping for the rest of our stay in Costa Rica. The next morning, we said goodbye to our hosts Maria and Jose (and, separately, to poor Diego), then popped in to see Jaime and Olga one last time for a cup of coffee. Grateful for our Nicoyan experience, we drove east to cross the grandiose La Amistad Bridge, which connects the Nicoya Peninsula to Costa Rica's mainland.

The wide and crocodile infested Tempisque River, which flows into the Gulf of Nicoya, is what kept Nicoya relatively isolated for centuries. Prior to the government of Taiwan funding the bridge's construction, less than twenty years ago, getting to Nicoya from the mainland involved either taking a boat, or traveling miles north to the nearest bridge followed by a journey through rough mountains back south to the peninsula. According to scientists, genetics account for about 25% of our individual longevity, whereas the remaining 75% is determined by lifestyle. Over the centuries, the gene pool in Nicoya remained mostly untouched, as its isolation allowed the indigenous people there to survive while wars and Spanish colonization affected the mainland.

***

Americans have been the most recent colonizers of Costa Rica and Galina and I were getting ready to meet two of them.

From Nicoya, and once we had crossed the river to the mainland, we drove south on Central American Highway 1, the Central American part of the Pan American Highway which runs from Prudhoe Bay, Alaska to Ushuaia, Argentina. We passed through San Jose, and then drove up into a mountain range to the town of San Jose de la Montana, to the estate of Wendy and Erich, along with their five dogs and two cats.

We received a warm welcome to their home, which is set on three acres of mountain forest with an expansive view of San Jose and its surrounding sprawl miles below, especially beautiful at night. The dogs, ranging in size from one of the smallest Chihuahuas we'd ever seen to an incredibly loving, and almost human, Great Dane, added a lot of life to the estate.

Wendy is a spiritual healer who sees fairies and other things most people don't, while Erich is a budding baker hoping to one day open his own bakery. They welcomed us to their secluded world in the mountains where, in the past, they ran spiritual healing workshops and retreats. But a recent financial loss, the result of an unfortunate bank fraud, had left them essentially penniless. They had no debt to speak of, and did own one nice car and a beautiful home, so they met the classic definition of "asset rich, cash poor." This was not, of course, the first topic of conversation, but this, and more about their lives, was shared over our meals together.

Wendy and Erich had moved from the US to Costa Rica fifteen years earlier, with children who are now grown up but still live in Costa Rica. Wendy had hoped, and planned, that the kids would settle down and make their homes nearby, but they put down roots a couple hours away, near the sea. This was a good lesson for us, and other empty nesters in general, about having expectations for our adult children. They can't be expected to follow us. The best we can hope for is that they will be happy to have us near them, wherever that may be.

Three acres of manicured gardens is a lot to manage, and there was a lot of outdoor work waiting for us. Wendy and Erich, despite their tight financial situation, still employed a full-time gardener to get the bulk of the work done. In a place like Costa Rica you can almost watch the plants grow, including the weeds. We were asked to weed several rows of bushes and, on Day 1, we got right to work. The next day, while Galina continued weeding on her own, I painted an outside wall of the house—another bit of tangible work where I could see the immediate result.

We ate three meals a day together, food that was always made from scratch, primarily by Erich. Given the tight financial situation, much of the food came from the garden, supplemented by good stocks of staple food which Wendy and Erich still had in the pantry. But we never were left wanting more to eat. It was only with time that we really learned the full extent of their current financial woes. Over each meal, which we all started with a deep and mindful inhale with our noses right up next to the food, we shared our respective life journeys.

I believe that, whether aware of it or not, we all carry past traumas throughout our lives, and Wendy made no secret of the traumas which impacted her. She was an unwanted third child, a fact that was made clear to her by her entire family as far back as she can remember. She shared about feeling hated and bullied by her siblings, and simply not feeling loved by her parents. She had a sad and, I suppose, even fearful childhood. This early path set her up for future trauma and unwanted life dramas, including a disastrous first marriage, from which she finally escaped years earlier, which produced her children. She then met Erich and, not long after, along with her children, they all moved to Costa Rica to start a new life together.

Wendy had written her life story some time ago and was intent on putting it into a book and getting it published. She had purchased e-book software but was having problems getting the final version ready for sale. She really wanted to sell her book and bring in some cash – even if it was only $10. I offered to do some research on the software and to figure out how to get the book published, and for the next few days I spent the afternoons inside the house working on Wendy's computer, proofreading the book and formatting it. Meanwhile, Galina enjoyed the meditation that came along with weeding. After a few days I had managed to get the book published for iBooks and Kindle, along with a small e-commerce site which allowed her to promote the book, *The Mystic Life*[iii], on Facebook. She sold a few copies over the next week, which gave me a real sense of accomplishment and, more than that, planted a seed in me that I needed to write my first book. I didn't verbalize this at the time; the seed was yet to sprout.

As the days passed, we were each able to connect with Wendy and Erich on a deeper and more personal level. We continued to share our life stories, recipes, and ideas for personal and spiritual growth in an authentic and open environment. We each came from quite different religious and spiritual backgrounds, and of course had vastly different life experiences, but we were all open to what each other had to share.

One evening Wendy announced that she and Erich had a gift for us—a bath together! No need to get undressed, however, as this was to be a sound bath. They escorted us to the sound healing section of the house and had us lay together, flat on a special bed. She and Erich then used various bowls and gongs to "bathe" us in sound for half an hour. The idea is that a sound bath sends you into a meditative state and, in the best case, on a journey of self-discovery and personal healing. I think I fell asleep (something I'm pretty good at doing in the horizontal position) and, while I recall it as a nice and pleasant experience, our true journey of self-discovery was yet to come.

In recent years, we had begun to hear stories from a friend or two about ayahuasca, an entheogen native to South America. An entheogen is, according to Wikipedia, a class of psychoactive substances that induce a spiritual experience aimed at either personal development or for a sacred use. I had already known a few people who had traveled to Peru and taken long hikes into the rain forest to meet with local shamans who would lead an ayahuasca ceremony. Each of the people who shared their experiences with me spoke of them having been profound and life-changing, or at least life-marking, moments. Not only was the journey to the location difficult, but the actual process of drinking the tea-like brew is not necessarily easy either. The ceremony is held throughout the night, during which time the dose taken invariably results in vomiting. This is a process which is meant to be both physical and spiritual, where one starts to face internal struggles or enemies, and experiences are usually reported as being a mix of terror and bliss. These usually end with some significant personal and potentially life-changing insights for each participant, although sometimes only after several consecutive nights of ceremony. I have met more than a few people in recent years who say their lives have been significantly changed.

Medically, the substance is not addictive and given the intensity of the process, it's usually not something for which people develop a regular habit or need. Also, the so-called "set and setting" for its use and maximum benefit, is extremely important and it is, therefore, not something that can be safely taken alone.

Prior to setting off for Costa Rica, we had done a bit of research on ayahuasca. It was starting to make its way out of South America, even though its practice was, and remains, illegal in many countries, including the US. But we had read about a medically supervised, and licensed practitioner in Costa Rica, and were intrigued by the idea of participating in a ceremony ourselves.

We started off by asking Wendy if she had any knowledge of ayahuasca, and it turned out we had come to the right place. She had taken part in some twenty ceremonies in recent years and knew about the place in Costa Rica we had read about, although advised against going there. "They cater to Hollywood celebrities and the like. No need to spend the kind of crazy money they charge," Wendy said. She was right, as it was essentially an expensive multi-day, high-end spa package.

Although could that really be so bad?

Wendy was willing to connect us with one of her own ayahuasca contacts (given she was obviously an expert), and at the same time suggested that, if we'd like, we could drink some "magic mushroom" tea one afternoon together with Erich. She thought this might be a better "gateway" to ayahuasca for us. Plus, she just so happened to have a few mushrooms in the fridge, left by some visitors a few years ago.

We felt convinced that Wendy knew what she was talking

about within the world of "woo-woo," and so we agreed.

Anyone talking about "magic mushrooms" is most likely referring to one of the many species of naturally grown mushrooms which contain the psilocybin compound. Psilocybin is a hallucinogenic similar in structure to the laboratory-created drug LSD. Neither are chemically addictive, nor are they highly toxic, which means that overdosing is virtually impossible. Physical dangers are generally limited to having some sort of accident when under their influence.

Galina had, up until this point, never experimented with hallucinogens, and neither had I—at least intentionally. A few years earlier while in Bali, I found myself, quite accidentally, on a psilocybin mushroom-induced "trip." I had been in Bali for several days on business, meeting some potential clients visiting from Mexico, together with my business partner, and was scheduled to fly home to Singapore that evening. The Mexicans had brought with them a gift in the form of two mushroom-laced chocolate bars, and left them for my partner without explaining that these were not simply bars of chocolate. My partner voraciously consumed the chocolate while at the same time offering me a small square, which I duly sampled. What soon followed was a three-hour experience of significantly heightened awareness of multiple senses.

Laying on a bed with my eyes closed, hand in hand with my business partner, I immediately understood where the inspiration for the psychedelic album covers of the Grateful Dead, and similar bands from the 1970s, had come from. Colors and patterns twirled like a kaleidoscope. I was keenly aware of my breathing in a way I had never experienced, even during meditation. There were even moments when I noticed, quite distinctly in my brain, that my breathing had stopped. Without a modicum of panic, I reassured myself, "Don't worry, you will start to breathe again soon." And I did. When I periodically opened my eyes, I could see a level of detail in ordinary objects near the bed which I simply would not normally notice, and I could succinctly hear sounds and conversations taking place outside the room, which in an ordinary state there is no way I would have heard.

All this while, at the same time, being aware that I had a plane to catch in a few hours, and also feeling a sense of sadness that I was having this experience without Galina. Those feelings didn't overwhelm me, but I have a clear memory of noting them, while at the same time continuing to let the uniqueness of the experience play out. In many ways this felt like I was experiencing a kind of ideal, deep meditation. The whole experience is difficult to put into words, yet once the effects had worn off, I immediately realized that this had been a significant event in my life. It was as though I had been visiting a parallel universe—one which I clearly know is and was always there, even in my normal life, and one which I had been given the opportunity to connect with for three hours. Much like while we sleep, the sense of time was not what it is during normal waking hours. What was, by the clock, almost exactly three hours, seemed on one hand like a waking eternity and simultaneously like a few short minutes.

I brought that significant life experience from Bali with me to an afternoon of mushroom tea with Galina, Wendy, and Erich. After we had completed our morning chores and eaten a light lunch, it was time to brew the tea. Wendy and Erich measured out what they thought would be a good dose for us "lightweights." We drank the tea together, left the cups in the kitchen, then each of us went our separate ways while we waited for the psilocybin to kick in. There was plenty of space in the large garden to first have a short walk, and to then lie down under a tree. Galina and I were within earshot of each other. Although the world felt to be at peace, for what seemed like perhaps thirty minutes nothing really happened. Galina was the first to report something was taking place. She could see design in the trees—a kind of order to the branches and leaves. Beauty. I began to notice the movement of the leaves in a way I don't ever remember. Then, almost at the same time, we both confessed to growing cold, perhaps once again due to the heightened sense of feeling, and one of us suggested that we head back to our room together. Unlike being drunk, we were able to walk calmly and in a straight line.

Back in our room, we both felt the desire to curl up together, fully clothed under the bedcovers, and this is where we would stay for what the clock would show to be a little more than two hours, but which for us felt like days. Periodically, we each came in and out of consciousness during this time and had quite different experiences. Galina, in her words, felt an overwhelming sense of love and of being loved. It was the love she had felt from her mother as a child, the kind of love we all long for. Disconnected from our normal cerebral functioning, she bathed in what she could only describe as God's love in a state of timelessness.

I, on the other hand, found myself facing monsters and grotesque creatures behind closed eyes. Absent were the beautiful shapes and keen sense of awareness of my breathing which I had experienced on my previous trip. This time something else was revealed—a new life lesson. The monsters would disappear each and every time I opened my eyes, something I felt very much the ability to control, yet I repeatedly felt the urge to shut my eyes and go back to the battle. The experience was not violent or particularly scary, just different from what I had experienced in Bali, and quite the opposite of what Galina was experiencing while snuggled up next to me.

As time progressed, the lesson the monsters wanted to teach me became clear. They represented several distinct areas in my life where I was taking on more personal responsibility than I should. I was vividly reminded of my so-called "Superman complex"—a desire to save everyone from every problem or difficult situation. This often leads me to take on too much and, at times, feeling as though I am carrying the weight of the world on my shoulders. As Galina and I—almost simultaneously—ended our trips, I felt lighter and more free than I had in years. I was able to specifically point out unnecessary responsibilities I had previously been feeling were mine to solve, and leave them in the mountains. Galina, who I would generally characterize as a nonstop, results-oriented achiever, was able to slow down and simply bask in the feeling of unconditional love. Neither of us knew what to expect before embarking on this experience together, yet both of us got what we needed.

Erich had emerged from his trip shortly before us and had made a fire upstairs in the living room. The four of us gathered to compare notes. Like us, Wendy and Erich had also had significant experiences. Wendy even remarked that she thought the afternoon may have been even more impactful than her previous experiences with ayahuasca. She went on to explain how connection with family and community is one of her core values, and also how she had just seen that she had been allowing her deep personal connection to their land there in the mountains get in the way of that. They had, of late, lived almost like hermits, allowing their connection to their property to keep them physically separated from members of their family, and from building any sense of community.

Prior to our visit, Wendy and Erich had struggled with the question of whether to sell their home in the mountains and downsize to one near the sea. They both had a desire to be nearer to their children and new granddaughter. Prior to moving to their mountain estate, they had lived by the sea and had loved feeling connected to the ocean. So while the desire to be connected with their family and to build community around them in the years ahead was pulling them away from the mountains, the emotional and spiritual ties they felt for their estate, not to mention the fairies Wendy sees there, were also strong and keeping them on the fence of indecision.

Although both Wendy and Erich each had their own separate mushroom-induced experiences this day, each came away with a similar message that they needed to take action to move toward the life they wanted. The next day they would relist their house on the market, lower the asking price, and get on with creating the life they truly desired.

By the next day we had both concluded that the mushroom experience we had shared together was sufficient, at least for the time being. We would pass on pursuing an ayahuasca ceremony in Costa Rica.

Prior to saying goodbye to Wendy and Erich, we took them out to dinner at a nearby restaurant. We shared beers together, the first alcohol any of us had drunk in our time together. Wendy had recently confessed that when we arrived, they had less than $100 to their names, despite having a Volvo SUV in the garage of their three-acre estate. Hence the relatively simple, yet delicious, meals we had enjoyed together without any frivolous consumption of beer or wine. We were happy to indulge a bit together in our final meal and to thank Wendy and Erich for sharing their lives with us.

Even though we had strayed outside the Blue Zone of Nicoya for this mountain visit, we agreed it was time well spent. It had also been time to make yet another memorable personal connection.

***

Despite the fact that it was time to move on from Wendy and Erich's place, we had not made any plans as to where or with whom we would stay next. Our intention was to head back in the direction of the Nicoya Peninsula, the "official" Blue Zone area of Costa Rica. We could see from the map that the Monteverde ("green mountain" in Spanish) region was about halfway.

"Let's go there!" Galina said, just as we were preparing to leave the house. She checked on Airbnb for listings in the area and her intuition, once again, proved invaluable when she found a homestay on a coffee plantation in the mountains, although the system showed them as having no availability.

"Somehow I think that's the place to stay," she told me. "Write them a message and ask if they have space for us."

I did just that, and within ten minutes we had a reply from Hermida telling us to come and stay for as long as we wanted. She said she had an extra room that she had not yet listed online. I replied that we'd be there in time for dinner.

Monteverde is still on Costa Rica's mainland (so technically not in the Blue Zone) but the Nicoya Peninsula is visible from many of Monteverde's high vistas, across the Gulf of Nicoya. The last ninety minutes of our drive gave us a taste of Costa Rica's infamously bad roads. This part of the country has only had roads (and electricity) for forty years. Prior to that, all transportation was on horse or by foot on trails. None of the mountain roads are paved, and some are intense, both in terms of road quality and sharp drop-offs with no guard railings.

Monteverde is also known for its cloud forest ecosystem and for having lots of rain, especially during the fall, which causes frequent landslides. Bridges and other stream crossings are often washed out. Unsurprisingly, the area feels a bit cut off from civilization.

It was this relative isolation which immediately gave us the sense that we would be able to experience a more authentic "Blue Zone" than in Nicoya where, in recent years, modernity has changed the way people live. Modern conveniences like paved roads and grocery stores stocked with Coca-Cola make for easier lives but less healthy lifestyles.

We were about to meet someone who embodies a Blue Zone lifestyle still today. Hermida, only in her sixties, manages her own coffee plantation, which includes two cabins she rents out to tourists. Like other foreign guests, we were immediately made to feel like members of her family.

As planned, we arrived not long after the sun went down, just in time for dinner which we shared with two other guests from America. After enjoying our meal of corn tortillas, beans, and chicken, all grown by Hermida and made from scratch, our host announced it was time for church and invited us to come along. We all agreed; the five of us walked together up the dirt road to the main village. I expected that we'd be attending the small Catholic church I'd spotted on the drive here, but we walked passed it (the lights were off there), and ended up on the second floor of someone's house. Moreover, our arrival for the service meant that the congregation had just doubled in size.

The service was led by a young Costa Rican, Jose, and his wife Jennifer. Jose led us in singing songs, which put my Spanish into practice, then preached a sermon. With our attendance, a significant portion of the congregation suddenly did not speak Spanish, so Jennifer became our translator. I guess they sensed I was participating well since, after the sermon, Jose asked me to say the closing prayer, which I did . . . in English.

After the service we spent some time chatting with Jose and Jennifer, who both spoke English fluently, about what they were doing pastoring this small church in Monteverde. These people are true believers and servants of God. They moved to this small village to start a church and be of service to the community by teaching English and helping the elderly. They lived a simple life and one they seemed happy and content to live.

Scientific evidence suggests that having a belief in God, or at least in something bigger than us, increases longevity. Not only does community often come with a belief in God through, for example, church or synagogue attendance, but also believing there are forces at work we don't control can help in coping with stress. While one can use religion as an excuse to surrender all personal responsibility for working to create the life one really wants, holistically, it is a fact that a religious or spiritual practice contributes to a longer life.

We stayed with Hermida for a week and usually ate breakfast and dinner with her. Each meal was cooked on demand and based on whatever she had fresh from her land. In addition to coffee, which she grew and roasted in an industrial-sized roaster next to her kitchen, she had all kinds of fruits and vegetables growing on her property.

In the words of her granddaughter, Hermida is a "tornado of activity," constantly busy with either cooking, roasting coffee, or organizing workers. Most are migrant workers from nearby Nicaragua, who either harvest bananas or plantains, or care for (and slaughter) pigs and chickens. She buys little from the supermarket; salt, rice, and oil is about all she ever needs to purchase. Virtually everything she eats is from her own or from a neighbor's farm.

On our third day, Hermida told us that we would need to cook our own dinner that evening, as she needed to pay a visit to her parents and spend the night with them. Hermida is one of sixteen children, all of who live in the area. The siblings rotate the responsibility of spending each night with their parents, a beautiful example of dedication and love. We, of course, asked if we could visit them, and Hermida agreed that we could drive her there that evening.

Before sunset, we drove Hermida to her parents' house, a journey which took less than half an hour by car, despite having to drive at a snail's pace due to the horrendous roads. Had we not driven her, she would have walked for an hour and half each way, up and down the hills and through the valley which separated their farms. Frequent and strenuous walking is another Blue Zone characteristic, especially in Costa Rica's mountainous terrain.

It appeared age had been kind to Hermida's father, Efrain, who at ninety-one still worked every day on his lush four-hundred-acre farm of rolling pastures with his three-hundred-head of cattle. Conversely, giving birth to, and raising, sixteen children in her lifetime seemed to have been hard on her mother, although she was still very much alive and alert at eighty-five.

After hearing him play a couple of songs for us on his guitar, we asked Efrain about the secret of his longevity. He was clear that hard work was key, not only providing physical exercise, but in alignment with the bigger picture of having a purpose for life each day. In his book, Dan Buettner cites this as the number one longevity factor in Costa Rica's Blue Zone—a *plan de vida*, or life purpose. Similar to the *ikigai* we learned about in Okinawa.

Keeping a focus on family came next in the list of Costa Rican Blue Zone longevity factors, and Hermida lived out this principle daily. Her own children, all adults, live in the area, including a son who lives with her at home. Born with obvious learning and developmental disabilities, he functioned well on the farm with daily chores, which included milking the cow. Hermida's love and dedication to him, and to her other children and grandchildren (who popped in for visits from time to time), was obvious.

Hermida also introduced us to her neighbors, Rosa and Rafael. After we had told Hermida why we were visiting Costa Rica, she knew we would like to meet this couple, both in their nineties. She told us more or less where they lived and how to get there so we walked about an hour the next afternoon from

Hermida's house for a surprise visit. We were welcomed, quite literally, with open arms. Galina's fluent Spanish came in handy as she and Rosa spoke at length about their families, and their smiles showed off their respective inner and outer beauty.

Connecting with Rosa, who was ninety-five, elicited the kind of authentic smile from Galina that is usually reserved for time spent with our grandchildren. Rosa was clearly an inspiration for living a long and happy life. She was in good physical shape, and the only medication she took was a small dose of an antidepressant, although she was happily unaware of what the medication was for. Throughout her life, Rosa had been a very social person, also deeply religious and active in her church. But in the last few years, her age had kept her mostly housebound, living in a simple home surrounded by a few immediate neighbors. Sadly, this reduced social interaction had brought her down emotionally.

Rosa and Rafael live alone and have a family-funded care provider who visits every day. She explained that Rafael, at ninety-four, had started to show signs of dementia, a sad potential drawback for some living to an old age.

The simple life we experienced with Hermida painted a beautiful picture of what, I believe, life would have been like fifty years ago throughout much of Costa Rica. This allowed us to get a taste of Blue Zone living in a part of the country subjected to limited influence from the modern world.

Leaving Monteverde, we drove back down the mountain roads to Route 1, which took us to the port city of Punta Arenas. From there, we took a two-hour ferry ride with our car across the Gulf of Nicoya, back to the Nicoya Peninsula where we would spend our remaining two weeks in Costa Rica.

Sitting on a bench on the deck of the ferry, and during a time when we seemed to be in a lull of travel planning, Galina suddenly said, "I'm still not sure about the glue." She was referring to the glue in our relationship and was obviously struggling in our mutual search to find a meaning to our relationship, now that we were empty nesters. Instinctively, my brain searched for some "quick fix" answer and I tried to come up with words to fill the awkward silence. Whatever I said didn't work and we soon found ourselves sitting out the rest of the ferry trip on different benches, each contemplating and processing what we would make of our future together.

Or whether there might even be a future together at all.

This was not what I expected, but we were in uncharted territory and Galina had spoken her truth.

***

There was, it turned out, also a fair bit of uncharted territory in the southern reaches of the Nicoya Peninsula. Recent rains had left some roads impassable, and we were told that Google Maps was not reliable enough to allow us to navigate while driving north to Liberia, from where we would eventually fly out. So after a few days in the south, we took the ferry back to the mainland, drove north on Highway 1 and, once again, crossed the La Amistad Bridge back into the northern part of the peninsula.

We wrapped up our time in Costa Rica by spending a few days with a local family who Galina, once again, seemed to magically find on Airbnb. The family lives in the town of Hojancha, which is not far from the city of Nicoya but sits at a higher elevation. It features in *The Blue Zones* as a center of longevity, so it was a town we wanted to visit before we left. We were fortunate to meet three generations there, and by staying on their family farm we saw how life was, and is now, for a friendly and extremely welcoming Costa Rican family.

Our room was in a recently built one-room casita which sat just between the cow barn and the original family home. The original house had been built by Alfonso, the family patriarch, more than seventy years earlier and not long before he and his wife, Carmen, married. They raised five children in that small, two-bedroom house, and even though it was no longer in the best of shape, it held so many memories for the family, they had no intention of tearing it down. They had built a more modern and slightly larger house right next door to the old one, about eight years ago, and the contrast was striking.

One morning, Carmen and one of her sons, William, showed us around the old wooden house. He shared his memories of the children and parents all speaking and joking together while lying in their beds before falling asleep. Although there was a wall between the parents' and children's rooms, it didn't extend all the way to the roof, so making conversation between the whole family was easy. Carmen's recollections of those days were primarily about "work, work, work," the only time they ever left the farm being on a Sunday to go to church. Otherwise, they worked from morning to evening.

Hard work—a recurring theme in our Blue Zone travels.

To me, the house served as a symbol of the core value of family that Galina and I were experiencing. Throughout Costa Rica, homes are built with patios that hold multiple rocking chairs on the front porch. Driving around Hojancha in the evenings we noticed how many of the porches were filled with multiple generations of family, sitting together on the floor or on rocking chairs. Notably absent was the glow of smartphone screens, which led us to believe that people were, most likely, actually *talking* to each other!

In the US, and in other wealthy nations, families with enough money, or borrowing capacity, tend to build large houses. In my experience, this can make it harder to stay connected as a family unit. Each person is able to do their own thing and, in effect, get lost in the space. Giving each child their own room is considered proper and almost a birth right for many children growing up in the modern world. But being intentional about building a smaller house, especially when children are young, might set a good foundation for strong family ties.

In Monteverde, we had seen how Hermida and her fifteen brothers and sisters took care of their parents, and here in Hojancha, we saw that, out of Carmen and Alfonso's five adult children, two had taken on the responsibilities of living and working on the family farm. William managed the livestock and rode his horse into the pastures every day, to round up the cattle for milking. One morning, while saddling up his horse he casually asked me, "Want to have a ride?"

"Why not," I replied. I jumped on and had a short ride about the front yard to prove that, like riding a bicycle, my horse-riding skills, learned at summer camp as a child in Texas, had not been forgotten.

The next day it was time to milk a cow, a first-time for me, despite our two-week stay on the dairy farm in Okinawa a few months before. In Okinawa, our main duty was dealing with what came out the cows' backside while our host handled all the milk production.

I tentatively grabbed a couple of teats and began to squeeze and pull down at the same time, fearing that this must be painful for the cow. William assured me that the cow is happy to have the pressure relieved and whatever strain I might be causing with teat squeezing was a price worth paying. After a few minutes, and not a lot of milk in the bucket, I also learned that, while being milked, cows are also able to produce a strong stream of poo—and the stream doesn't fall far from the milker. I jumped off my milking stool and ran away to avoid the splash, all to the delight of William and Galina who looked on. That was pretty much the end of my milking career as William then took over and, within seconds, extracted more milk than I had in the course of several minutes.

After almost two months in Costa Rica, the time had come to fly back to Houston, to see family and to take on our first pet-sitting assignment before a planned trip to Asia on business. As we drove from Hojancha to Liberia, there was silence between us as we both reflected on our time spent in our second Blue Zone. Since we didn't have any immediate plans to make, we simply didn't have much to speak about. There were still more Blue Zones to visit in the new year, so the question of what we would do with our lives once this adventure was finished remained one we could put off answering. For now, this was our *ikigai*, our reason to get out of bed in the morning each day. But this lifestyle was neither sustainable, nor, we were learning, good for longevity. It became clear that, in time, we would need to commit to becoming part of a community and, ideally, create a life where multiple generations of family members are nearby. Staying together as a couple would likely help with that—another elephant in the room with which we both struggled.

But then there was Hope.

HOPE

"They say a person needs just three things to be truly happy in this world: someone to love, something to do, and something to hope for."
- Tom Bodett

HOPE CAME AS A DOG. She was a "rescue" from Thailand, whose current owner had found walking alone and mangy, on the beach while on holiday in Phuket. When entrusted with her care in Houston, the day after we returned from Costa Rica, she was already eleven years old. She was a smart dog—smart enough to know that all her basic needs were met, and all she really needed to do was sit on the couch all day and wait for her next feeding. Hope may well have been more active earlier in her life, but now in her waning years, she apparently no long felt the need to be out and about.

Hope was the first dog we took care of using our TrustedHouseSitters membership. Our staged photos with dogs and carefully curated stories of our own household pets had earned us a week with her while her owner went away on holiday. By now we had also been selected to sit for two cats in Singapore, another step in building up our track-record as successful pet-sitters, so that by the following summer we would be able to fill our calendar with pet-sits in the UK. Our plan was starting to come together, although right now, as a minimum, we simply needed to keep Hope alive.

We arrived at Hope's home—a one-bedroom unit in an

upscale apartment complex near the Galleria area of Houston—at the time agreed with her owner. We were welcomed, shown around, and after about fifteen minutes of chit-chat, including a review of feedings and all things dog care, were given the keys and free rein over the house. We considered for a few moments just how unlikely it was, on the surface at least, that someone could invite strangers in to their home and, after fifteen minutes, leave them there for days on end to look after a family member. The power of the shared economy.

Houston's Memorial Park was located a short distance away. We like to take long walks and had assumed Hope would be happy to join us. On day one, we loaded Hope into the car, in itself a red flag as she needed to be lifted onto the back seat after refusing to use her own strength to jump in. The weather was cool as we started off on what was to be a three-mile loop around the park. Hope was a bit slow from the beginning, but aside from a moment when she simply sat down under a tree and refused to walk for about ten minutes, we made it around the loop. A few days later, however, it would be a different story.

Galina's militant style of getting me to exercise and eat right over the years had paid off well in terms of my physical health, and she was ready to apply the same rigor to Hope in order to get her moving. The weather was warmer on this Saturday afternoon and we once again hoisted Hope into the car and headed for the park, intending to walk the same three-mile loop. Slow to begin, we managed to pick up the pace a bit and, about halfway through, stopped at a doggy water station for Hope to rehydrate. She drank well and we started again, but after a few minutes she simply stopped and sat down, right in the middle of the walking path. This was a popular trail for Houstonians, so joggers and other walkers (some with and some without dogs) passed by regularly. Hope was panting and seemed a bit tired, so we waited a few minutes. But this time, instead of standing up to walk again, she dropped down to all fours. After about a minute, she lay down on her side and shut her eyes—right in the center of the busy trail. Until now, only a few of the passers-by had paid any attention to the dog resting on the trail, but as soon as Hope was lying down, eyes shut, more and more people stopped to see if she was all right. "She's dehydrated," one lady said, and pulled out a water bottle and started to pour it into Hope's mouth. We knew that Hope had just drank some water, so we didn't fear dehydration, but by now I was feeling more than a little worried and told Galina that I would run back to the car, then drive back to collect them. As I hurriedly made my way, thoughts of having to call the owner and apologize for killing Hope had my heart racing. The whoop-whoop-whoop of a helicopter overhead suddenly had me worried that someone had called "Life-Flight for Dogs" (not even real a thing) to rescue our dying dog, a clear sign that irrational fear had taken over.

Once I had retrieved the car and driven to a parking lot not far from where I had left Galina and Hope, I could see them under a tree and Hope was, to my delight, sitting up. Galina told me about the spectacle of help being offered in my absence and it did seem that Hope had been a bit overheated and simply needed to rest.

Naturally, that was our last "long" walk with Hope, and no, we didn't mention this little incident to her owner when she returned a few days later. Hope was happy, the apartment was clean, and we left fresh flowers and muffins as a way of saying thank-you *and* also as a small bribe aimed at getting a good review from the owner, who would remain blissfully unaware that we had come close to pushing Hope too far.

A few days later we received our first 5-star pet-sitting review.

***

Halloween was approaching and we had now successfully visited two of the five Blue Zones. We still had seven months to accomplish our goal of experiencing all five, but were beginning to have second thoughts about how much time, if any, we wanted to spend in Loma Linda, California, the only American Blue Zone. Our daughter had lived in Southern California for several years and knew of Loma Linda. "You'll be bored out of your minds there," she told us more than once. Also, I somewhat question the authenticity of Loma Linda as a Blue Zone. It is, after all, a much more modern settlement than the other four locations, whose longevity histories date back centuries.

Loma Linda is to Seventh Day Adventism what Salt Lake City is to Mormonism, as a large portion of the city's residents are practicing Seventh Day Adventists. Given that adherence to a religion is common to all the Blue Zones, and that Seventh Day Adventism is a protestant branch of the Christian faith that advocates a plant-based diet, it's unsurprising that many of the documented longevity cases in Loma Linda are of people following a vegetarian or vegan lifestyle.

Galina and I had, for several years, heard about the health benefits of abstaining from, or at least eating less, animal protein, consumption of which is tied to heart disease and cancer. I resisted moving my diet in that direction for a long time but, after years of struggling with an elevated cholesterol level, I began experimenting with how going vegetarian or vegan affected my numbers. It turned out that I was able to reduce my cholesterol levels (specifically, the LDL measure of so-called "bad" cholesterol) significantly by following a vegan diet. I don't characterize myself as a vegan, which in the strictest sense would mean consuming no animal products at all, such as not wearing leather shoes. I prefer instead to refer to my diet as "plant-based." Since Galina and I were already fully up to speed on vegetarian and vegan lifestyles, we didn't feel a strong need to visit Loma Linda. We had driven through the city a few years prior when visiting California, so we would be able to say we had, in fact, visited all of the Blue Zones, even if based partially on a technicality.

Even with our originally planned visit to California shelved, we still had two more Blue Zones to visit—Sardinia, Italy and Ikaria, Greece. Both are islands in the Mediterranean Sea where the weather during the winter months can be rainy, windy, and cold. It was now fall with winter just around the corner, so we were in no rush to head there for now. Besides, time was still on our side.

From Houston we flew, via Singapore, to Bali. I needed to check in with my office and attend a board meeting at Green School, my main business project at this time and one on which I was still working, even on our travels.

Although we had a clear plan of visiting the Blue Zones during this year of transition to becoming empty nesters, we were still quite lost as to what our lives would look like when finished. Or where we'd be.

We continued to think that settling in England made sense, even if for no reason other than to enable Galina to eventually apply for a British passport based on my British citizenship. But we had just discovered that the UK had quite strict immigration and naturalization rules. While getting *residency* for Galina wouldn't be too difficult, obtaining citizenship was a completely different story. To become a citizen required that we be physically present in the UK for the vast majority a period of more than six years, which felt almost like a prison sentence. None of our children or grandchildren currently lived in the UK and tying ourselves to that geography for so long didn't feel right. Ironically, given the fact that the UK was still part of the European Union (EU), and despite the Brexit vote which had taken place a few years earlier, we could quite easily apply for residency in Spain. Galina could accompany me there as my spouse and, after ten years, apply for citizenship without the onerous physical presence rules which applied in the UK. Spain now looked like a good place to visit *and* to establish residency, if nothing more so that Galina could have the freedom to move around the EU without the need to apply for visas on a regular basis.

We had spent most of November in Asia, where we expanded our TrustedHouseSitter track-record by taking care of some cats in Singapore. One of the cats was owned by a young professional couple without children, who had completely spoiled their beautiful long-haired Persian feline by hand-feeding it, piece by piece, with wet cat food. We had been instructed to coax the cat to us by opening a can of food, taking a small piece and putting it in the palm of our hand. We then had to play a kind of "cat and mouse" game of chasing the cat around the apartment and waiting for her to finally come and eat each piece of food, one by one, lapping each piece with her sandpaper-like tongue from my hand.

What in the world was I doing with my life, chasing someone's cat around an apartment trying to feed it?

I had limited patience with this game and knew that the cat wouldn't die of starvation over the few days we were there, so in the end the cat was subjected to a bit of intermittent fasting.

From Singapore we flew to Spain, where Nicholas was now in his second year at university. He was in the ancient Roman town of Segovia, not far from Madrid, and this was to be our first stop in Spain where we planned to spend most of December. We had arranged another pet sit in the south, near the seaside town of Malaga, and drove there from Segovia, to the home of a retired British teaching couple and their very loving—albeit not very smart—dog named Fitz.

As was becoming normal with our pet sitting experiences, we arrived the day before the owners were scheduled to depart and shared a meal with our hosts. Peter and Maria had purchased their retirement home in these Spanish hills a few years before retiring. During their international teaching careers, they spent a number of years teaching in Singapore, which, we would learn over dinner, was why they chose us for the sit. They felt a connection with us when they read in our profile that we had spent six years living there. Post-retirement and now in their late sixties, they had settled down to a relatively quiet life in Spain. Peter played golf twice a week and took care of the house and pool, while Maria volunteered teaching English to children.

This area of Spain has a lot of British and other European retirees as permanent residents, so Peter and Maria had been able to make some friends. Their two children, and grandchildren, lived in the UK, where they were going for a visit while we took care of Fitz. They expressed some concern about how much longer they would be able to keep living in Spain, considering that their immediate family was not nearby. Some early indications of health concerns also made them wary about how sustainable life, in relative isolation, might be. Due to a leg problem, Maria was no longer able to comfortably scale the hill behind their home on foot. Galina and I were reminded of our new friends in Costa Rica wanting to move closer to their children as time was moving on. Retirement in exotic locations, such as Spain and Costa Rica, might sound lovely, but age becomes something to consider. The older one gets, the harder it is to move. (Food for thought as we consider where to live as we get older.)

Peter and Maria left the next day and we would spend the next two weeks living in the hills and taking daily walks up to the walled city of Comares, which had great views of the countryside in one direction and the Mediterranean Sea in the other. On clear mornings, we could look out to the sea and watch the sun pop up over the horizon, just as we had in Okinawa a few months before.

It was in Spain where Galina would, almost overnight, find her "calling" in life. Or so it would seem...

Wherever we are, we always like to find local markets to buy vegetables and other fresh food, and Spain was no exception. We turned up one morning to the weekly market, a mix of Spanish farmers selling produce and British expats selling everything from jewelry to haircuts. On one stall we found a middle-aged British man selling, of all things, knife sharpeners. I'd been hearing complaints from Galina for years about dull knives in the kitchen, and given we didn't need any jewelry or a haircut, we started a conversation with Michael, the knife-sharpener man. Michael impressed us with his sharp knives, and sold us on the sharpener itself, while at the same time talked to us about his career as a professional chef. He had worked in restaurants in London and had also worked as a personal chef for several families. Unbeknownst to me, this had set a spark of curiosity alight in Galina. The next morning, after walking Fitz, Galina and I sat down for a coffee in the local village and she told me she now knew what was next—for her at least. She intended to enroll in Le Cordon Bleu's professional chef training course in Paris. She would start as soon as our summer in England was complete. That would allow her to become a private chef and travel the world. Exactly where my own career fit into these plans wasn't quite clear to me. And that was the point – at least for the time being.

So now there was no longer any doubt about what we would do when our Blue Zone travels were finished. Either that, or perhaps we'd simply managed to kick the can down the road yet again as to what, or to where, we would commit. Other than vagaries about becoming a private chef or working internationally in hotels, Galina could not articulate clearly what it was she *really* wanted to do with the qualification once the course was finished. But she would have a degree, and this would allow her to embark on a professional career – if she would want to.

In hindsight, it became clear that Galina was looking for some certainty in life beyond what we had at the moment. My professional path, at the time, was far from certain. The effort I was leading to expand Green School beyond Bali was still in its infancy. This entailed raising investment funds to pay the salaries of a team, which would include me, and although we had secured some investment to get started, funds were coming in slowly. There always seemed to be another key date just around the corner that would determine if the project would continue or not. Although Galina and I both knew I could, in theory, find work anywhere in the world, there was still a high degree of uncertainty as to which direction my career might take us. The question of where we would live, and around what we would base our day-to-day life, still loomed large. Add the question of purpose, that we both dealt with as empty nesters, and it wasn't a real surprise to me that Galina would want to enroll in a program like Le Cordon Bleu, which would "force" us to live in Paris for about eighteen months. Plus it gave Galina a tangible option for financial independence, if necessary. She wanted some assurance that she could make it on her own if she had to.

We passed our time in Spain and traveled back to Houston on Christmas Day to spend time with family, before returning to Spain in January to continue residency formalities. We had also been selected for two new pet sits in the south of France, just across Spain's border.

It is scientifically proven that pet ownership improves longevity. Pets provide companionship and a reason to get up each day, since the pet relies on its owner to survive. Pets can help with an *ikigai* at a certain stage in life. One week in January we found ourselves taking care of a twenty-two-year-old cat, Nina, in Thuir, France. We worried that Nina might die on us during the sit, but her owner assured us that she'd had a good life and, if that were to happen, they wouldn't hold it against us. Before leaving for her holiday, the owner told us "Don't worry if she dies – all I ask is that you put her in the deep freeze so that I can properly bury her when I return." Fortunately, Nina outlived our stay.

Cats are much less work than dogs and it struck me one morning, while looking after Nina, that the only reason I had to get up that day was to feed her. For years it had been my duty, and joy, to get up each morning before school and prepare breakfast for our boys. I would almost always sit with them while they ate, even if we were all too sleepy to speak. At times I would go back to bed for a bit more rest before getting on with my day, but I had a clear sense of purpose as the day began. Of course, I didn't get quite the same sense of satisfaction from Nina, but I was aware of the needs which she and I were fulfilling for each other *that* day.

By February, after jumping through further residency formalities, we were on our way to becoming permanent residents of Spain. Never mind that we currently had no real intention of *living* in Spain, but the fact that we could if we wanted to, gave us a feeling of certainty which we both appreciated.

Galina had recently been complaining to me that she felt overly attached, or tied, to me. No one wants to feel forced to be with anyone or be anywhere, as it goes against our basic human desire of self-determination. She relied on me not only for money, which is common for women who choose to raise a family as a career, but also for where she lived or was able to travel to. A Russian passport holder was still not particularly welcomed in most Western countries, at least without going through the bureaucracy and sometimes humiliation of applying for a visa. European countries were notorious for only issuing visas for short periods, so getting a European residency card, valid for five years, was a big help.

Adding insult to injury, Galina's driving license had expired several years before. "Another reason I'm stuck with you!" she angrily told me one afternoon, while walking two Labradors in the south of France. We agreed then that we would prioritize a trip to Moscow for her to renew it.

Beyond the need for the added sense of freedom that would come from having a valid driver's license, there was one more reason to visit Russia that winter. This was the year both Galina and I would reach our 50th birthdays. Halfway to one hundred. We had, for several years, talked about chasing the northern lights as a fun way to celebrate and Russia seemed like an appropriate place to do that.

We did some research and discovered that the far north of Russia is one of the best locations to get a chance to experience the northern lights (or the *aurora borealis,* as they are known scientifically). Murmansk is a well-populated city far above the Arctic Circle, where it gets sufficiently cold throughout the winter to have many days with limited cloud cover, an important element in being able to see these astronomical phenomena. The other necessary ingredient for a proper sighting is sufficient solar activity in the atmosphere, enough to generate the ionized particles that cause this beautiful show of nature. The northern lights get the most press and sightings, but the southern pole also generates the same activity on the bottom side of the planet. However, more people, infrastructure, and even land mass exists in the north.

We agreed that in between Blue Zones we would make a trip to Russia to renew Galina's driver's license and to attempt to see the northern lights.

It was now late January, and we were moving between Spain and France, taking care of some pets and, in general, passing time until we made our next Blue Zone visit to Sardinia in March. We checked the website of the Russian tour agency that would be our host in Murmansk. They had posted information on predicted solar activity for the coming two weeks, as provided by the Russian weather service, as well as forecasted temperatures. You need both high solar activity and extremely low temperatures (at least - 20 Celsius, or below zero in Fahrenheit) to have the best shot at actually seeing the lights.

At the end of the month, we saw what looked like a great window of opportunity, with predicted high solar activity combined with forecasted temperatures of -30 Celsius. At that temperature clouds tend to break up and the sky is usually clear. Thankfully we weren't looking after any pets at this time, and quickly set our sights on getting to Russia.

Madrid-Moscow-Murmansk was our flight route in early February as we left Spain. We were surprised that more than half of our fellow passengers on the flight from Moscow to Murmansk were Chinese. It was Chinese New Year at the time, and we soon learned that a trip to see the northern lights had been quite fashionable in China in recent years. It also seemed that some creative tour guides were helping to perpetuate a myth that it was good luck for a couple to conceive a child under the northern lights, and that child would be rich. We were initially told this was an ancient Chinese belief, but given that the lights are not generally visible in China and that it has only been a few years in the course of human history that Chinese, or much of humanity for that matter, has been able to travel outside their homelands, we concluded that this must be a fairly new "belief," one which the Russian tour companies selling tours to the Chinese, were happy to offer.

Murmansk was founded in 1915 as a supply port in World War I, due to its strategic location, and is Russia's only seaport with unrestricted access to the Atlantic Ocean. It sits at the tail end of the gulf stream, which means that, despite frigid temperatures during the winter (it was -35 Celsius when we arrived), the Barents Sea does not freeze. This makes Murmansk one of the world's northernmost year-round ports. It is also the largest city on Earth above the Arctic Circle, and host to the world's most northern McDonald's. Coal, timber, and other products are shipped by rail into Murmansk and then off to warmer climates by boats sailing above Norway and into the Atlantic Ocean. Murmansk is also a port of departure to sail to the North Pole in the summer on one of the few commercial ice-breaker ships.

Our plane from Moscow landed around noon, only about an hour after the sun had come up. In early February, Murmansk gets about four hours of sunlight each day and people are starting to come out of their sun-starved winter depressions. Quite literally, every local we chatted with over the next few days commented on how difficult it is to live in this climate during the winter months. Yes, it's cold, but the absence of light is more difficult to deal with. In December, there are days when the sun does not even rise. People use sun lamps to help ward off depression, but Russia's *main* tool for dealing with such despair is vodka, which seems to do the trick, at least temporarily. Of course, in the summer the "polar nights" turn in to "white nights" when the sun doesn't set at all, so life here is extreme—and tough on the body.

It's no accident that the Blues Zones are all located in much more moderate climates.

A couple of hours after we landed in Murmansk, our tour guide called to tell us that the excursion to see the lights was on for that night. To see the aurora borealis, one needs to get away from the light pollution of the city and drive at least an hour into the countryside. Throughout winter months the tour company monitors the weather in the region to determine the best place to have a chance of seeing the lights. Assuming the weather cooperates, the tour company then informs its clients that a night-time excursion is on.

For our excursion, we were to meet at the hotel lobby at 8:00 p.m. where a bus would take us, along with about twelve Chinese tourists, to a viewing spot in the countryside. We drove to a World War II memorial an hour or so outside the city, parked by the side of the road and were told that we would wait to see if any activity would start. Nearly fifteen minutes later, with almost impeccable timing, our guide announced that a show had begun. He invited us to climb the small hill to get the best view. We could see waves of what looked like gaseous clouds form on the horizon and, with time, they became more pronounced and rose higher into the night sky. Our guide had a camera and immediately began to organize the group for photos. It was then that we learned the reality about what is seen with the naked eye versus what the camera sees.

We had noticed the gaseous movements in the sky and could make out a bit of greenish color on the horizon, but so far what we had observed was nothing like what we had been used to seeing on TV or in photos. But as soon as our guide showed us the display screen on the back side of his camera, we were amazed at what the camera recorded. We had just learned a fact which most people don't know about the northern lights. Most of what is seen in a photo or video of the lights is not actually visible to the human eye, because at night our eyes are unable to pick up most of the colors that a camera can. So, while the camera proves that the colors are real (no Photoshop or filters were involved), it's mostly just the streams of gases in the sky which can be seen with the naked eye. But the experience of being in this wonder of nature was awe-inspiring, even though most of the colors are only visible in photos.

We spent a couple of hours watching the show, shuttling between the snow and the hot tea available in the bus. Being outside was very, *very* cold, and despite wearing six layers of clothing, the only way to prevent freezing was to move—jump, walk, run. Keep moving or freeze to death. Much like in life, so even here in Russia, we were reminded of one of the Blue Zone lessons: *keep moving or die.*

Over the next couple of days, we took a drive to the Barents Sea and spent a morning visiting a tribal village. But our most memorable outing, aside from the lights, was a visit to a team of Alaskan and Siberian huskies—a dog team which actively competes in sledding competitions. We were introduced to these beautiful dogs whose genetic makeup apparently doesn't allow them to bite or harm humans. We learned about the roles different dogs play in their sled teams. The more intelligent leaders, though often not necessarily the biggest or strongest, are at the front, while the ones with the muscles and strength are at the back, closest to the sled.

It was a beautiful thing to see the dogs put into their designated spaces, and to then see how excited they became as they prepared to run . . . jumping up and down, barking and pulling on their reins in anticipation of what it was they were about to do. The energy was palpable, and we could feel their joy from the moment the sled was let loose and the dogs were allowed to run. They pulled and ran with all their might, doing what they were designed to do. It was a beautiful thing to witness.

I felt a sense of awe watching this team of beautiful animals so joyfully live out their purpose of hard work and service. Yet another reminder to keep a focus on purpose and on what brings joy in life, and another necessary reminder to us that we needed to find that purpose beyond our own travels. We still had two more Blue Zones to visit, which would be followed by a summer of pet-sitting in England, and Galina had now signed up for professional chef training in Paris starting later that year. So if nothing else, we were filling up our calendar.

Sardinia was next.

SARDINIA

"Determine never to be idle. No person will have occasion to
complain of the want of time, who never loses any."
- Thomas Jefferson

SARDINIA, PART OF ITALY, is a rocky island in the Mediterranean
Sea, to the west of Italy's mainland and just south of the smaller
French island of Corsica. It is one of Europe's oldest civilizations,
populated ahead of Italy and well before the Roman Empire. Given
their long history with foreign invaders, Sardinians are generally
wary of outsiders, and this is likely one of the factors driving
longevity there. It would also make it more difficult to connect
with locals - more difficult, by far, than we had experienced in
other Blue Zones.

We traveled to Sardinia by boat, which felt like an authentic
way to get to an island with such a history. Native Sardinians,
who are genetically more akin to Spanish or north Africans than
Italians, survived foreign conquests over the centuries by moving
up to the mountains, where the terrain and weather is harsher than
on the beautiful coasts. They adapted to these tough conditions,
which kept them away from the foreign invaders who couldn't be
bothered to chase them in to the hills. This also likely served to
thin the gene pool of weaker links.

We had returned to Spain from our Russian adventure
and found a somewhat regular ferry service running between
Barcelona and Sardinia. After a twelve-hour ferry ride across the
Mediterranean, we arrived at the minute port city of Porto Torres,

located on the northwest tip of Sardinia. We had booked ourselves a small apartment in Alghero, the largest city in the region, with a population of about 45,000, and a history that goes back to the 8th century BC. It grew as a city about two-thousand years later, after the arrival of colonists from Catalan (now part of northern Spain and southern France, where native Catalonians continue to this day to fight, sometimes violently, for their independence). The Catalan language is still officially recognized in Alghero's region in Sardinia, although Italian is spoken by everyone, and Sardinian, or Sard, is spoken by native Sardinians. The Sardinian language is generally considered the closest living language to Latin. *Who knew?* I certainly didn't.

As with our previous Blue Zone visits, we arrived in Sardinia with no real plan of how we would go about experiencing the place. Getting there was the first step and we had done that. We spent the first few days walking the cobblestone streets, visiting shops and the local market. Quiet prevailed at that time of year. The city's population usually increases four- or five-fold during the summer months, but it was now the end of February and cooler temperatures kept people away.

Walking around town on our first day, we saw a sign in a shop window advertising a weekly qigong class, scheduled for the next day. Qigong (or "chi gung" to some) is an ancient Chinese breathing, movement, and meditation practice with a strong historical tie to martial arts. We messaged the phone number on the sign and received a reply inviting us to attend the following day. The class was held in Italian and we followed along with the slow and simple movements as best we could, thankful that the other attendees showed grace to us first-timers.

The teacher, an Italian who had moved from Milan to Sardinia with her husband twenty years earlier, to escape city life, invited us for lunch at her home the next day. We walked about an hour outside the city to her house in the country and met her husband, Marco. We had a nice afternoon chatting, but we were still a bit lost in terms of grasping our purpose for being on Sardinia. We seemed to be just wandering—much like in our life in general—looking for a sense of where we belonged and a reason to get up every morning.

We would, however, soon have a reason to move on to other places on the island as our son, Marcus, was flying to Sardinia to spend some time with us. A bit like us, he was on his own gap-year and had just finished spending two months in South America, living in hostels and hiking. Being with us, he would be taking a break from living on a shoestring, backpacker's budget. Marcus flew in to Cagliari, the capital city of Sardinia in the far south, about as far away from Alghero as one could get on the island. We rented a car and drove to meet him, still not knowing exactly where we would end up in the weeks to come.

Sardinia is well-known in tourist circles for its beaches, but we knew it was the inland, mountainous areas which held its longevity secrets. Specifically, it was in the Nuoro province of Sardinia where the "Blue Zone" name was conceived. Dan Buettner first visited Sardinia in 2004, after hearing about a cluster of villages in the mountains whose inhabitants shared a rare genetic marker—the M26 marker—which researchers believed was correlated with longevity. Various scientists in the past had studied this marker, and this area's isolation had allowed the gene pool to stay intact.

Dan and his team set out to gather statistics on the number of centenarians in the region; they found nearly ten times the number of centenarians per capita when compared to the United States. While planning their visits to the various villages, his team had a map on which they used a blue pen to circle the names of villages with the highest number of centenarians. It was from that map, with the villages marked by blue circles, that the term "Blue Zones" started to be used.

We did not intend to be overly scientific or specific as to the villages we visited, nor did we have any sort of connection to the region in terms of getting introduced to people. We would simply make things up as we went along, and decided the Nuoro region was where we'd head next. Airbnb had, so far, proved to be a good way to meet local homeowners, so we started there. There weren't many listings on Airbnb in the Nuoro region, especially within a reasonable driving distance from Cagliari. Still, we found a place with an English-speaking owner in the small mountainous village of Meana Sardo, and while it was nice to have a host who spoke English, it turned out that she was actually living in Canada. She did, however, have a niece who would bring us the key and let us in to her small stone house.

Meana Sardo was a typical Sardinian mountain village with narrow, stone streets and houses built side by side, with no sense of town planning other than all buildings emanated outward from the central church. Even though they were built over the centuries, they remained more or less in the same style.

We arrived at the house a bit earlier than planned and parked out front, by the gate, hoping the niece would soon arrive. Our car blocked the entire street as we waited, but there was no regular traffic for us to interrupt. After a few minutes and exchanging text messages with the niece, who said she'd be there in about half an hour, an elderly lady poked her head out of the house next door. Sensing we weren't dangerous, she approached us to offer assistance. She wore a black dress, black blouse, black sweater, black shawl, and black boots, contrasted by a green kitchen apron tied around her waist.

Maria would be our next door neighbor for the next few days. She was quick to invite us in to her house while we waited for the key, and through a combination of broken Italian and some similar Spanish vocabulary, we learned a bit about her.

Maria was ninety and had been a widow for a number of years. She lived alone in her own house during the days but spent every night in her son's house nearby. We had read that Sardinia doesn't have retirement homes and that families take care of their elders until the end, and here was an example. Much like Costa Rica, the importance of family, and specifically how elders are respected and taken care of, is a key part of life in Sardinia.

We entered Maria's simple home while she jabbered away about her family and children. She offered us coffee but was a bit off in her well-meaning attempt as she put the coffee pot in the oven instead of on the stove. Our key showed up before the coffee ever appeared.

The niece with the key knew Maria well and was in some way related. She apologized for being late and for allowing us to have been "captured" by Maria, then showed us in to our tiny—and cold—stone house. Relieved of our bags, we decided to walk to a restaurant or bar for a coffee. As we walked into the street Maria was there once again, apparently curious to know what we were doing. We invited her to come with us for a coffee. "No, no, no," she said. "I can't do that. That's not allowed." As a widow, at least in this part of Sardinia, Maria is required to wear black whenever she is outside the house, and is not allowed to be seen with other men.

There were no other foreigners staying in Meana Sarda, and it didn't seem to be a place which would attract many, even during the summer months of high tourism. We spent a few quiet days in the town. The local grocery store was somewhat reminiscent of shops in Siberia during the 1990s, boasting mainly bread, pasta, canned goods, and alcohol.

Life is simple in this part of the world.

We walked around the quiet streets and experienced another similarity with the Blue Zone of Costa Rica: hills. The mountainous terrain means residents constantly walk up and down, even as they walk around town. Before cars, villagers would have to walk from town to town to trade their goods and walk into the hills to tend their sheep.

Over the next few days, and as we planned our next stop, Maria knocked on our window from time to time, just to make her presence known. Not wanting to travel too far, we once again used Airbnb and found our next stop, a place in the small village of Paulilatino, a couple of hours away from Meana Sarda.

Chiara, our young host, not only offered us a home in which to stay, she and her mother also gave cooking lessons in her home. We signed up the following day. While mixing semolina flour with water and salt, we talked about life in Sardinia. Chiara had left her small village after school and attended university in Rome. She then became a flight attendant for a European budget airline, but after having worked for a few years, decided she wanted to come home to family. Her mother did not yet require special care, but Chiara knew the time would come when her presence would be needed.

We made a local pasta, *malloreddus,* small gnocchi-type pieces of dough made from semolina flour. Semolina is a grain that is a "resistant starch," making it a healthier alternative to pasta that is made from traditional wheat flour. Resistant starch doesn't turn into sugar in the small intestine, but rather moves on to the large intestine, where it ferments and promotes digestive health, including supporting the immune system. This might well be a longevity factor in Sardinia, where semolina is prevalent.

Once each of us had kneaded our semolina-based dough, we proceeded to make thumbnail-sized pieces of pasta, one by one, and rolled them out on a special corrugated piece of wood—

kitchen gear apparently found in all Sardinian kitchens. Chiara explained that getting together with friends or family to make malloreddus is a common tradition in Sardinia, combined with another social activity—drinking wine.

Sardinian wine, made from the locally produced cannonau grape, has been credited as also being a longevity factor. Not only does wine, in general, aid in bringing people together socially, the cannonau grape, grown on Sardinia and one of the most popular varieties on the island, apparently has health benefits above and beyond regular red wines.

The cannonau grape is a late-ripening variety which, thanks to the hot, dry climate, develops a thick skin, leading to it having a higher concentration of polyphenols than typical red wines. Polyphenols are micronutrients contained in different edible plants, especially those with color such as cacao (used to make chocolate) and berries. Polyphenols are widely known to have all kind of health benefits, including a possible reduction in heart disease, thanks to their "artery-scrubbing" characteristic, which is why it's often said that red wine, in general, is better for you than white wine—it's the polyphenols.

Whereas generally around the world, women tend to outlive men, Sardinia is a Blue Zone which seems to endow longevity to men and women equally. Maybe this is due to the cannonau wine of which, according to Dan Buettner, two glasses tend to be consumed each day by males in Sardinia. Although it's also worth considering that most people are often less than truthful in admitting the amount of alcohol they consume, so it may well be that this "longevity wine" plays a bigger role than even Dan gives it credit for!

In the middle of our cooking class with Chiara, a gentleman— likely in his seventies— paid the family a visit. He had come to have lunch with Chiara, her mother, and some other family friends, but first came in to say hello to us. Alessandro was, apparently, a well-known veteran journalist in Sardinia. We explained why we were visiting his island, and that we didn't actually know where in Sardinia we would be going next. He immediately recommended that we drive up into the mountains of Barbagia to visit the town of Perdasdefogu. There, he said, we would find an authentic Blue Zone mountain village. His cousin rents out rooms in her house there, so he immediately phoned her to let her know we would be coming the next day. Yet another serendipitous encounter which would point us to one more memorable experience. (I have nothing against advanced planning, but we were seeing yet again how setting a general goal and moving toward it, while letting the details unfold on their own, makes for a fun ride. This is a lesson that can be applied to many different aspects of life.)

The mountainous Barbagia region of inner Sardinia received its name from the Roman statesman Cicero, who described it as a "land of barbarians." The area was never fully conquered or ruled by the Romans, as these tough, local people made a life for themselves over the centuries in the harsh, rugged environment. The ancient Romans went on to describe the Sardinians from this area with a Latin term meaning "thieves with a rough garment in wool." That history remains in their DNA today and must, I believe, play a role in their longevity success.

Driving up to Perdasdefogu took several hours and, once we got into the mountains, we saw what a rugged physical environment this was, and would have been, in an era before modern roads. Alessandro had told us to be on the lookout for two villages, which were now ghost towns following an earthquake that had made them both completely unsafe to inhabit. We couldn't miss them and what an eerie sight they were. Two villages, each visible from the other, across a deep valley, both abandoned about fifty years earlier. Street signs still marked the roads, while kitchens and bedrooms now stood exposed to the elements as most of the roofs had caved in.

About an hour later we arrived in Perdasdefogu and eventually found the home of Alessandro's cousin. She welcomed us and helpfully pointed us in the direction of one of the few open restaurants. We had at least found enough common ground with our Spanish and her Italian to get ourselves fed. We ate well, drank some more cannonau wine, and did our best to speak with the waitress and explain why we were visiting. She immediately mentioned the bar nearby which she, and others, refer to as the "Longevity Bar."

We visited the bar the next day, and upon entering understood where its unofficial name had come from. On one wall hung an official Guinness Book of World Records certificate that read:

> The highest combined age achieved by nine living siblings is 837 years and 6 days and is held by the Melis siblings (all Italy) of Perdasdefogu, Italy. The achievement was verified on 20 June 2014.

The Melis siblings had actually been on a bit of a record-breaking streak previous to 2014. They were first noticed and recognized by the Guinness Book of World Records as the longest-living group of siblings on earth several years earlier. Each year that passed added nine years to their impressive record. However, in 2014, one of the siblings died and the current official certificate proudly on display at the time became the final one to have been issued.

Another frame hanging on the wall displayed a 2012 article in the Guardian newspaper entitled "Sardinian Siblings Credit Minestrone Soup for World Record Age." The bar's owner, Alfonso, was quoted in the article as saying, "We eat genuine food, meaning lots of minestrone and little meat and we are always working." He went on to say, "Every free moment I have I am down at my vineyard or at the allotment where I grow beans, aubergines, peppers and potatoes." To say that they have a history of eating local would be an understatement.

I went to the bar to order a round of longevity drinks—espresso for now—and asked the middle-aged bartender if Alfonso was around. "He's at church," the man replied, which made sense given it was a Sunday. It turned out that the bartender was Alfonso's son, Marco, who managed the bar. Alfonso, at that time, was ninety-six. I asked Marco what he believed to be his father's secret to a long life. "Hard work!" he exclaimed, without giving my question a second thought.

For me, this visit to Alfonso's "Longevity Bar" turned out to be one of the most impactful experiences of our entire Blue Zone journey. Although Alfonso no longer managed the bar, he remained very much the owner and, I believe, felt relevant and useful when he showed up. So long as he can move, there will always be something he can do at his bar, and someone there to listen and speak to. For Alfonso, owning his own bar gave him a purpose, or *ikigai*, which he can live out, on his own terms, until his final days.

Many of us find relevance and purpose in our jobs, and I am no exception to that. In the world of business, I have noticed how executives often start to become less relevant and less effective the older they become. Above a certain age, some degree of slowing down becomes inevitable, and even the healthiest and best-intentioned senior citizens can struggle with keeping up with change, hence the role of mandatory retirement which many large companies impose on their employees and leadership. This makes sense for the company, but what then happens to the retiree and how do they find purpose once their career is over? Some succeed at finding something new while others struggle.

In Perdasdefogu, however, Alfonso had both a job and purpose which will work for him until the very end. His duties evolved, and will no doubt continue to evolve as certain limitations manifest themselves and body parts and functions run past their warranty period. But, as the owner, he is not subject to mandatory retirement and his job is one which keeps him connected to people and doing something useful, even if only polishing wine glasses.

So Alfonso and his bar had me thinking and planning for what I will refer to as my "final third" in life. What is it that I can do that will have a high probability of giving me control over my own sense of daily purpose, my *ikigai,* for the last portion of what I hope will be a life of about one hundred years? From my sixties I want to be in a place where I can do just that, be it opening a bar, coffee shop or my own cheese business ("Saye Cheese" has a nice ring to it!).

We spent a few days in the area, driving through many of the small mountain villages, and took one long drive down to the nearest coast to get a sense of just how remote the Blue Zone villages are. We then said goodbye to our host and headed for what would prove to be the antithesis of Perdasdefogu.

***

Porto Cervo is the modern, ultra-posh yachting Mecca of Sardinia, located on its northeast coast. We had visited this resort town years earlier, where we watched wealthy Russians and the like board their boats with staff dressed in matching uniforms. We had taken an afternoon pleasure cruise with some other tourists, and our captain pointed out a yacht owned by Russian oligarch and Chelsea Football Club owner, Roman Abramovich.

There was a stark contrast between the vacation homes, villas, fancy shops (all the Italian luxury brands have boutiques in Porto Cervo) and high-end restaurants of Puerto Cervo and

Perdasdefogu, where we had just spent the last few days. Porto Cervo is a place where people come in the summers to be seen, show off and to indulge in the "good life."

And then they leave.

We had arrived in March and the area reminded us of the ghost towns we had passed through a few days earlier, albeit here the roofs were still intact. Virtually everything was closed, yet in another month or so, the place would buzz with the rich and famous, and many more who wished they were.

We spent one night in a condo, which had an expansive view of the Mediterranean. The wind was strong and the sea itself full of waves. We would sail back to Barcelona the following day from Alghero, the port town a few hours drive away, where we had first made landfall in Sardinia. But before that, a final meal was in order. All restaurants close at this time of year, so we found a grocery store and bought all that we needed to make *malloreddus,* the pasta dish we had learned to make a week earlier with Chiara in Paulilatino. Accompanied, of course, by a bottle of cannonau wine.

The following morning, before driving off for Alghero, I took a walk alone down to the beach and found a large rock to sit on and watched the waves. For me, watching waves roll to the shore calms the chatter in my mind—a bit like meditation and maybe even more effective. I reflected on where Galina and I were in this particular journey, but also on where I was in my own personal journey of life. In a week, I would turn fifty—halfway, God-willing, to becoming a centenarian.

After visiting three of the five Blue Zones, we were realizing that the older residents in those places had, to one degree or another, all lived what most would describe as a "hard life." None were wealthy, at least in monetary terms, and all seemed to live somewhat in isolation and in locations where physical labor was a necessary part of life.

I believe that very few people would, if given the choice, choose a hard life over an easy one, even if it meant being granted additional years to live. Being honest with myself, I knew I would likely choose to be a yacht owner in Porto Cervo rather than a shepherd in Perdasdefogu, but what does that say about me and what I value?

I had finally started to scratch the surface of what I wanted to make important in the second half of my life. I didn't know it at the time, but after visiting three Blue Zones, something was starting to get through, and I was starting to ask myself what I wanted from life and why.

From what we had seen and experienced on this journey so far, it seemed Blue Zone residents, at least the older generation, had very few choices in life. They simply never had the opportunity to move to another country, or even move to the city. Perhaps some could have moved away but, for whatever reason, they chose to stay, and their roots grew deep. Their core values were formed, and they lived according to those values.

In a world where we have seemingly infinite choices and options, from what we eat, to our profession, to where we live, and to whom we marry or stay married, I believe that identifying our core values becomes all the more important. Only then are we able to live our lives and make conscious choices that are consistent with those core values.

I believe our core values are not things we choose for ourselves; they are part of us. They are primarily God-given, or pre-programmed through our DNA, and then nurtured from an early age by our primary caregivers, as well as our environment. Our core values are who we are.

Sardinia was the first place where this started to sink in for me. The life we had been living for more than a decade was one characterized by having a lot of choices. Rooted in the desire to give our boys a unique, global education, we had chosen to live in five different countries over ten years. This had worked out as intended in regards to the boys' education, but it also left us without roots, and inadvertently, had turned us into a kind of global gypsy couple. Ironically, traditional gypsies have life expectancies anywhere from ten to fifteen years *less* than the general population, and yet here we were studying longevity in the Blue Zones.

***

We drove from Porto Cervo through the northern mountains of Sardinia and back to Alghero, where we dropped off our rental car and then caught a bus to the port. Mediterranean ferries are notoriously late, and this was no exception. But we were not in any hurry to get anywhere right away.

The ferry would take us back to Barcelona in about twelve hours. We needed to be in Bali in a month's time for some Green School meetings, and had arranged a pet sit in Dubai—a convenient halfway point—in early April, about two weeks away.

Before all that, however, was my fiftieth birthday.

Our intention was to spend a week in Jordan, a halfway point between Spain and Dubai. We hadn't yet booked flights or hotels, but there would be time for that once we got to Spain and had put Sardinia firmly behind us.

HALFTIME

"The real measure of your wealth is how much you'd be worth if you lost all your money."

- Unknown

GALINA AND I MADE A PACT a few years earlier that we would no longer give each other physical birthday gifts. Instead, we would make our giving based on experiences, which in general evoke emotions in a stronger and more meaningful way than what we feel when given a "thing." Not to say that receiving a nice piece of jewelry doesn't create a feeling, but the feeling tends to be more fleeting and, in my view, less memorable than what comes with an experience. The things in life we remember the most, good and bad, tend to be associated with experiences we've had.

As if traveling to the Blue Zones over a year was not enough, we decided that while we were at it, we should truly binge on amazing travel experiences. We had previously set the goal of seeing the northern lights to mark our 50th birthdays, which we'd accomplished a couple months earlier. But now that the actual birthdates were approaching, mine first in March, we looked on the map for a memorable place to be when I hit this milestone.

There are not many places in the world that we have visited where we long to visit again. This world is so large and there are so many places we have not yet experienced that returning to a country feels, in general, a bit like a waste of time. For some reason though, Jordan (officially The Hashemite Kingdom of Jordan) is, for us, an exception. We had visited the country twice since we married (once with the kids, once without) and it left a strong impression on us. Jordan's history spans such a long period of time that it somehow puts our lives into perspective. The daily, visible reminders there of ancient sites and ruins going back to the times of both the Old and New Testaments, help me let go of worry about life's problems or my professional goals. For me, these kinds of places help to put our speck of a life into perspective.

There was also a practical element to choosing Jordan, it was a convenient halfway point between Spain and Dubai, where we had committed to spend ten days looking after a cat.

Jordan has always occupied a strategic position in the world, located at the crossroads of Europe, Asia, and Africa. The Dead Sea serves as part of its border with Israel, as does the Jordan River, and the site of where John the Baptist was baptized. The river is a popular tourist destination and pilgrimage site for Christians. Jordan also has a port city, Aqaba, on the Red Sea, and sixteen miles of Red Sea coastline, giving Jordan shipping access to the world. Despite sharing borders with Saudi Arabia, Iraq, Syria, Israel, and Palestine's West Bank, Jordan has for decades been a land of relative stability in the region. King Hussein of Jordan served as king from 1952 until his death in 1999. Since then, his son, King Abdullah II has reigned the country as a benevolent dictator, which seems to have served the country well. He and his father have allowed literally millions of refugees over the years to live in Jordan after fleeing regional conflicts.

On our previous trips to Jordan, we visited many of its famous tourist sites, including the baptism site of John the Baptist, Amman's very impressive Roman ruins and Mt. Nebo, the mountain top believed to have been the spot where, in the Old Testament, Moses looked out into the Promised Land before he died. But this time we chose to focus solely on our two most memorable spots in Jordan: the Dead Sea and Petra. We would spend a week in Jordan and split our time between these two sites.

Petra is a world-renowned UNESCO heritage site, and in 2007 was named one of the "New 7 Wonders of the World." For me, as a childhood fan of Indiana Jones and the Raiders of the Lost Ark franchise, Petra's notoriety came from the Al-Khazeh, the massive Greek-styled temple carved out of the face of Petra's trademark red sandstone. The Al-Khazeh was used to represent the entrance to the temple housing the Holy Grail, in the third and final Indiana Jones movie, *Indiana Jones and the Last Crusade.*

We landed in Amman in the evening and were driven by car to our hotel, a two hour journey to Wadi Musa, the town adjacent to the Petra site. Petra is Jordan's most popular tourist destination, and Wadi Musa has grown over the years to support the explorers and, more recently, tourists, since the site was discovered in the early nineteenth century.

Petra is a massive site, in total over a hundred square miles, and even the bits which tourists can visit take several days to cover. More than two thousand years ago, Petra was an entire city of desert-dwellers. The Nabateans no longer exist as a people group, but for a period they were quite a wealthy and successful civilization. Utilizing their strategic location, their wealth came from trading incense with camel caravans moving between the Mediterranean and Red seas and from Egypt to Greece. Before the Romans came and took over around the time of Christ, what is now Jordan was, for many years, part of the ancient Greek empire. The Greek influence is the most prominent at Petra, first and foremost in its name: The word *Petra* means "rock" in Greek.

Petra boasts the remains of an ancient irrigation system (complete with underground storage caves), which was used to support a population of 30,000 people living in a dry, mountainous environment. But it is the tombs and caves carved into the red stone walls of the mountains which are most notable at Petra. They come in all sizes, from small cave openings into what were presumably small homes, to massive, ornately carved reliefs which apparently served as the tombs of the nobility. This is where the Greek influence is most visible, with classic, triangle-shaped pediments topping Corinthian columns. The sunlight adds to the magic as the red stone changes color throughout the day. The entire site is one giant work of art.

The Roman's influence was also left in the form of a giant, 6,000-seat amphitheater, as well as the ruins of an early Christian church. Petra faded into obscurity after an earthquake in AD 336, and the advent of Islam a few centuries later. It was discovered in 1812 by a Swiss explorer and, over two hundred years later, more than half the site is yet to be excavated[iv].

This was our second visit to Petra. We had come to Jordan thirteen years earlier, with our children, while we lived in Moscow. Unsurprisingly, there were many more tourists this time, and most were Chinese. From the entrance to the site in the town, a short car ride from our hotel, it takes about an hour to walk to the Al-Khazeh. The first half of the walk is down a dusty road where most people, us included, reject repeated offers for an over-priced ride to the site by horseback or donkey. At the end of the road we entered the Siq, a windswept and picturesque ravine of red sandstone, which was obviously a main entry point into Petra. Both sides of the ravine are lined with the remains of an aqueduct system, which brought water in from higher elevations. The ravine walls quickly become pretty high and it gently slopes down to an opening, where the massive Al-Khazeh (the height of a ten-story building) suddenly comes into view. The entrance to Indiana Jones' Holy Grail temple!

Beyond the iconic Al-Khazeh, the spot at which many tourists turn around and head back to their busses, there are hours more of hiking available. We spent two days on the site and managed to hike on a few trails where we passed only the occasional tourist. It was there, on my 50th birthday, that I was able to reflect on the past decade of my life.

In the thirteen years since our last visit, nothing had changed with the red Petra sandstone cliffs and carved out caves, other than the busloads of Chinese tourists visiting the site daily. While the desert, rocks, and stones had remained the same, I reflected how so much in my life *had* changed.

Over the past thirteen years we had lived in six different countries, and our children had all grown into functional adults, each pursuing their own dreams for life. I had woken up to the fact that I needed to change my diet to maintain good health. Simply put, I had been eating too much meat, bread, and sugar, and by cutting down significantly, or almost eliminating these, I had lowered my "bad" cholesterol level and lost ten kilos (twenty-two pounds). I had previously been blind to the fact that I was overweight.

But my biggest blind spot had been my relationship with money and how the pursuit of it had prevented me from being my true self and from living in accordance with my values. The fear of being a financial failure had driven my actions, and often inactions, over the years and had me stuck, preventing me from even knowing what I really wanted from life.

Over the course of two days in Petra, I reflected on my life's journey, much of which could compare to the search for the Holy Grail. Indiana Jones had found it in Petra, maybe I could as well.

The concept of the Holy Grail dates to King Arthur and the middle ages. Various traditions describe it as either a cup or stone, with miraculous powers that provide happiness, wealth, and abundance. That was certainly what I had been striving for in my own pursuit of money over the years. Money had not only brought security but, more importantly, self-worth in ensuring that I would not be a financial failure.

***

I was thirty-seven when we had last visited Petra. A year later, and almost overnight, I found myself wealthier than I had ever thought possible. Shares in the company I had been working for were suddenly worth millions, thanks to the oil and commodity price boom of the mid-2000s. Natasha had just graduated from high school in Moscow and was heading to the US for college. Our boys, Nicholas and Marcus, ages nine and seven st the time, were ready to transition from a Russian school to one that taught in English. Growing up in Russia, the boys had not been able to spend regular time with my parents in Houston, who were now getting on in age. All things considered, it felt like it made sense to cash in my chips and move to Houston. The boys could attend school there, we would be in the same country as Natasha, and be near my parents. And I now felt rich. My fear of financial failure was now gone.

Or so I thought.

For years my aim had been to avoid financial failure by making a lot of money. Yet I had never actually set a goal for myself as to how much money would be *enough*. Nor did I give any thought to what I would *do* with my life if I did, in fact, get *enough*. In hindsight, I think I never really believed I could get to that stage anyway, so why bother planning for it? I was content to live my life in fear of financial failure and planned accordingly. I would spend my entire life working, trying to make enough money to feel like I wasn't a financial failure, and then I would die. Suddenly, at the age of thirty-eight, I found myself with a net worth beyond any goal that I might have set or imagined possible. Somehow, I felt that this was in fact now *enough*, but I simply didn't know what to do.

Be careful what you wish for.

While living in Houston, I turned forty, an age meant to symbolize the halfway point in life. Turning forty can be a great time to evaluate one's life and consider what the second half will look like. I made a feeble attempt at doing this by picking up a copy of *Halftime*, by Bob Buford,[v] a book specifically aimed at helping the reader move from the first to the second half of life. Specifically, he writes about moving from "success to significance."

I'm ashamed to say that, although I started the book, I never actually finished it. It just didn't resonate with me, namely because I was still stuck in my dysfunctional relationship with money. I simply wasn't able to stop and take the time to really consider what I wanted to do in life and how I could best use my talents. A quote from the book reads:

"My passion is to multiply all that God has given me, and in the process, give it back."

Very aspirational, but not something I could get my head, or heart, around in the slightest. My focus was to turn my millions into more millions, even though I still had no clear idea, goal amount, or reason why. Perhaps by doing so, I could finally prove to myself that I was a serious entrepreneur, truly worthy of my gains, and then somehow go on to have more than the elusive *enough* that I had been chasing all these years. For me, the measure of *net* worth was a measure of *self*-worth, and this is how I would invest my time—and money—for the next few years.

Money was my focus and my identity. My fear of being a financial failure had been a key motivator for being on my professional path for the past two decades. As soon as I became "rich," the fear of financial failure should have, in theory, disappeared. But it didn't. It had simply evolved from being a fear of not having enough money, to a fear of losing what I now had, as well as a fear of not being able to make more. In truth, my fear of being a financial failure was much more about the shame I would feel from losing my money and what others would think of me, than not having enough money to provide for my family, which was never a concern. It was all about me. My ego was driving me to earn more money to boost my self-worth. I could justify it all by saying it was for my family, and there certainly was some truth in that; in my heart I really do want to provide well for my family. But the fact was I simply wanted more. I believed that "more" would take care of my fear.

Fear causes one of two reactions—either running away or freezing in place. I had reacted in both ways. Now that I had money, the fear of losing my wealth led me to pursue several high-risk investments and business ventures, most notably drilling for oil in Siberia and chasing an oil contract in Turkmenistan. I rushed into these endeavors with the primary aim of making more money, while at the same time conveniently creating a false identity for myself as a swashbuckling oil man. These ventures failed, and my net worth took a hit. And because my self-worth seemed so intrinsically tied to my net worth, my self-worth began to suffer as well.

Aside from my failed oil ventures, professionally I basically did nothing. I bought a Range Rover and BMW and focused mostly on maintaining my image as a successful and independently wealthy person than pursuing anything of meaning or creating value for others. I dabbled in a few investments in the stock market, with mediocre results at best. The real issue was that I remained rudderless.

Schooling for the boys provided a legitimate and well-intentioned purpose, which would take us from the US to Europe, and then to Asia. All the while I remained, for the most part, under-employed and without a clear purpose or direction in life.

Five years after leaving Russia and taking on my new image as an independently wealthy oil man-cum-investor, we ended up in Singapore for the boys to attend school there. We would stay in Singapore for the next six years as the boys went through high school.

Although I had more than enough money to live comfortably, I did not have any real purpose or direction in how I was living, and by the time we moved to Singapore my net worth had started to sag. A couple of bad investments hadn't helped matters, but the main issue was we were spending more money than I was earning on my investments. At forty-three, with two children still in private school, university tuition around the corner, and now living in one of the world's most expensive cities, the math just didn't work for us to continue living as we were. The financial status quo was not sustainable, and it was time to get back to work.

In a way, I believe I had subconsciously brought this on myself. I essentially set things up to lose money so that I could have a reason to work and avoid being a financial failure, and then the cycle could repeat itself again. This perverse, subconscious logic, after five years of dabbling, brought me to the point of setting out to work once again.

Fortunately, the start of work that would become meaningful and fulfilling came across my path, even if I didn't quite recognize it at the time.

During the course of our school year in Bali, I met John Hardy, the co-founder of Green School. We had enrolled the boys for a one-year "eco-education" in the Bali jungle. This wall-less school was made entirely of bamboo with a curriculum built around educating for sustainability. John is a visionary and tireless promoter who, along with his wife and co-founder Cynthia, conceived the idea of a school that will raise up a generation of green leaders. They had spent most of their lives committed to beauty, primarily through jewelry. John moved to Bali from Canada in the 1970s, where he later met Cynthia. Over the years they built a wildly successful jewelry brand together—John Hardy. They exited the business in 2007, and then proceeded to put money, time, and energy into creating the school.

Green School was truly a thing to behold, as John and Cynthia believe that children simply learn better in a beautiful environment versus being locked inside a concrete box. The school opened with just under a hundred students and has since gained notoriety on the world stage for its unique approach to holistic education, thanks largely to John's endless and passionate promotion of the concept at global events like TED.

When I met John, he needed help managing his financial life, both related to Green School and various other ventures in Bali in which he and his family were involved. This included a bamboo design and construction firm, a boutique hotel, and a number of real estate investments in various stages of development. He asked me, more than once while we were living in Bali, to consider helping him bring oversight and order to all this creativity, parts of which could certainly have been described as chaotic. "I feel like you are someone I can trust," he told me after our second meeting. I resisted, mostly out of fear, but John persisted.

We moved to Singapore just in time for the boys to start at United World College of Southeast Asia, which would take them through high school over the next six years. Within weeks of moving to Singapore, the reality of living in one of the world's most expensive cities, a dawning decade of international school fees and university tuition, combined with my deteriorating net worth, prompted me to realize it was time to get busy making some money.

John contacted me again to ask for help. I agreed to give it a go and made the first of what would be countless trips between Singapore and Bali, providing oversight and management for John's "green world."

I rented a small office in Singapore's Central Business District and hired Glenn, an accountant, to help me get started. About six months later, I partnered with a former colleague to formally establish the MarcWhittaker family office. Salman and I had worked together years earlier in Azerbaijan. At the time, I had just established the Baku office for Arthur Andersen (the global accounting firm which would be taken down by the Enron crisis a few years later). Just like now, I needed a tax expert to help me serve clients and Salman was sent to me from the London office of Arthur Andersen. Now he was available to help me once again.

Although our primary focus in the years to come would be acting as a fiduciary for John and providing oversight of Green School, we also helped a handful of other entrepreneurs establish and manage their businesses and financial affairs in Singapore. This helped pay the bills, but I still carried around a huge amount of fear and anxiety about my personal finances. What if I could not earn enough to cover all the family expenses? What if I ran out of savings? I could feel the fear in my chest every morning.

My first step in really waking up to the reality of my fears, and finally taking action to face them, came on a family vacation in Mauritius. Although we had been living in Singapore for less than a year, it was enough time to have done the math and see that my net worth was falling by the month. And with a mindsight of this being tied directly to self-worth, I was living in a constant state of fear and did not feel good about myself.

In Mauritius, every dollar I spent seemed to raise my anxiety level to a point where something had to give. One afternoon, in a brief moment of solitude, and without any prompting, I sat in a chair, shut my eyes, and gave up. In that moment I decided I would simply allow myself to face the fear of financial failure. There and then, in my mind, I gave myself permission to lose all my money and all my income.

Within a few seconds, in my mind I was completely broke and my deepest, darkest fear had come to fruition. Nothing in my bank accounts, and creditors calling to say I owed them money. My wife had left me and my kids now knew that I had become what I feared the most: a financial failure.

As horrible as that sounded, and as scary as it was to go there, I soon felt an overwhelming sense of calm. While just like in a country music song, I had no money, no wife, and no house, yet I also felt free. Finally, I was free of the fear that I had been trying to keep at bay all my life. As I looked around at my life in that moment of extreme fantasy, I realized I was still me and still alive. I had breath, a beating heart, and two hands, which I could now use to rebuild my life; I could make it, even if I were alone and broke.

That spontaneous mental exercise created a shift in my psyche and opened the door to a new way of being and relating to money. It wasn't as if, from that moment on, I suddenly stopped worrying about money, but it marked the beginning of a journey of personal development which would start to unfold in the years to follow.

I continued to slowly build my firm, MarcWhittaker, while traveling often to Bali to meet with John and help oversee Green School.

In Singapore, I started to build other client relationships, including a few guys via previous connections in Russia and Kazakhstan. These were wealthy people. When I had made my money in Russia few years earlier, I thought I was rich. Yet, compared to the people and circles I now found myself in,

I quickly realized how relative wealth is. These almost daily interactions with people who had been more "successful" in life than I, at least financially, slowly chipped away at me as I constantly compared myself to them. Why had my investments not worked out like theirs? Why hadn't I worked in Russia longer and saved more money?

In short, why wasn't I more like them?

I drenched myself in guilt and made myself the ultimate victim. If I was going to move forward and get out of my current negative feedback loop, I needed to rebuild myself and start to take responsibility for my life.

About a year after my Mauritius epiphany, I found myself in an intensive two-week personal development training program in Singapore. AsiaWorks has its roots in the teachings of personal development legend Jim Rohn, to whom Tony Robbins attributes much of his life work. A number of quotes are attributed to Rohn, but one which applied to my situation at the time was, *"If you don't like how things are, change it! You're not a tree."*

The AsiaWorks group training was an active, highly confrontive, experiential two weeks where all the excuses and victim stories I had made up for my life were exposed. I was in a place of complete honesty where I gave and received feedback about how I and my fellow trainees showed up in life. These two weeks were a significant inflection point in my life and marked a new way of how I would interact with others. It's not an overstatement to say that I would never be the same again, experiencing more love, more openness and honesty, including an openness to being wrong.

As humans we long to be right about whatever it is we believe, and search for clues and evidence to prove that we are right. If I believe that my boss is an idiot I will find and latch on to every bit of evidence that proves they are an idiot. If you believe you made the right call about an investment you will work to convince yourself you are right, even in the face of evidence that the investment was bad. Furthermore, if the investment finally proves to be a failure, you will likely find someone else to blame and make yourself the victim, failing to take ownership for the wrong decision.

The training revealed this exact pattern in my life and the intensity left its mark, raising my awareness of how I had allowed these patterns to sabotage my life and my success.

So much changed after those two weeks. I related differently to my family, my clients, even to strangers. One exercise in the training required me to approach a random person on the street, engage in a meaningful conversation and "break bread" together, all without ever revealing this was being done as part of a training.

God, I believe, led me to an African American man wandering around a mall in Singapore. I approached him, struck up a conversation, and we ended up sharing a meal together in the food court. Jake was a US Navy employee, who worked on a Navy ship which had docked in Singapore for a few days. During this "random" meal I shared with a stranger, he spoke about struggles he was having with his wife and children back home. I hardly said a word, and it was apparent that my role was to simply listen, a lesson for other relationships perhaps. For that short period of time, we connected as two humans each with vastly different backgrounds but with common needs.

The relationship I had with my soon to be son-in-law would never be the same again. Renado, also an African American, had come into our family a few years prior when he fathered our first grandchild. Galina and I viewed Renado as an arrogant, entitled millennial. Natasha claimed that she loved him, but it was not something we wanted to hear. Their relationship flew in our faces in terms of racial stereotypes and the social "norms" which both

Galina and I had both been conditioned to. I failed, however, to give any thought to my own situation, twenty years earlier, when I had married a Russian with a child from a previous marriage. This, I know, required acceptance and love to be shown by my own parents, but this was the furthest thing from my mind when it came to me being able to accept Renado and Natasha's relationship and "out of wedlock" child.

Like many parents, we had our own plans and ideas for what Natasha should do with her life, and a seemingly random guy she met at a Starbucks was not part of our vision (as if any vision she might have had for her own life even mattered). Up until then, we had held on to our convictions about Renado not being right for Natasha, unaware of our own deep-seated, fixed beliefs about what we thought was "right". There was talk of marriage, and more children down the road, yet we resisted, refusing to see how their values and backgrounds could align.

My training, and specifically sharing that meal with Jake, had taken me out of my comfort zone and showed me that I could in fact connect with anyone. *Anyone.* I immediately began a new chapter in my relationship with Renado. When I opened myself up to the possibility that there may in fact be an authentic and deep connection between them, I could see their relationship in a different light. Ironically, the fact that we had raised Natasha in different countries and cultures, and the fact that she was a product of parents from different cultures, made her a "minority" in the United States, a label which could also be applied to Renado in America. They had, I believe, at least in part through this, found common ground on which to build a strong and meaningful relationship.

Later that same year I walked Natasha down the aisle at their wedding ceremony in Bali. I certainly no longer see him as the arrogant, entitled millennial – an image that I had created in my mind based on my own prejudice and *my* arrogance.

It seems that each generation finds a way to challenge the former generation's stereotypes and social beliefs. Upon reflection, I had done this with my parents and Natasha (and Renado) did the same with me. With the pursuit of longevity will come the need to adapt to societal changes and regularly assess certain long-held ideals, especially as I plan to be around for multiple generations.

For me, the AsiaWorks training was, quite simply, life changing. Going forward, I saw the potential in others and in myself which I had not seen before. And I stopped comparing myself to others.

Most importantly, however, I now realized that it was entirely my responsibility to create the life and the kind of relationships I wanted. I now knew that virtually any relationship has the potential to be a positive one if I want it to be, and *if* I take responsibility for it. Gone from my vocabulary was the phrases "he is so…" or "she is so…"—words of judgment that immediately shift blame to the other person and make me the victim of their behavior or actions.

With my newfound sense of confidence and love for others I began living differently. A few years later I discovered I could pass on much of what I had learned and practiced through personal coaching. I completed a professional training program and started to incorporate the process into my family office and financial advisory work.

***

Upon reflection from the rocky terrain of Petra, the six years we spent in Singapore were, for me, years of incredible personal growth. I could see that I "grew up" in Singapore, so maybe I had found my version of the Holy Grail here in Petra after all. Fifty years into life, halfway to being a centenarian, I had started to connect the dots of my life purpose for the second half. Perhaps I could then go back to Bob Buford's book and, at last, find it relevant.

After two days in Petra, we drove north to the Dead Sea, where we spent a few days simply floating in the salty, buoyant water twice a day and enjoying the peace and quiet of a five-star hotel with a sea-view room. Ten days in Dubai was next, where we looked after a cat for a couple who were teachers away for their spring break. We celebrated our twenty-second wedding anniversary in Dubai with afternoon tea and Champagne at the Burj Arab, overlooking the Persian Gulf, before heading to Singapore and Bali for some work commitments.

Our next Blue Zone stop was finally around the corner.

IKARIA

"If more of us valued food and cheer and song above hoarded gold, it would be a merrier world."
- J.R.R. Tolkien

DAN BUETTNER PUBLISHED THE ORIGINAL Blue Zones book in 2008 and has since sought to expand the Blue Zones concept and brand. As an offshoot from studying longevity, Dan later decided to look at happiness and see what life lessons can be learned from the world's happiest people. *The Blue Zones of Happiness* (National Geographic Society, 2017), actually identified Singapore as one of the happiest places on earth.

Singapore made the happy-place list due to the strong sense of security its residents feel. It has one of the world's lowest crime rates and, as a society, Singaporeans have willingly exchanged a degree of personal freedom for feeling safe. This was one of the main reasons we chose to live there while our boys went through high school. Bringing drugs into the country is punishable by hanging and lesser crimes are punished by caning. Irrespective of one's views about human rights, this acts as a strong deterrent to crime.

Safety and security are, arguably, at the top of the list of basic human needs. Nothing else really matters in terms of being fulfilled as a human being. By combining a culture of low crime with a social safety net provided by a financially strong government, Singaporeans, by and large, feel safe and secure.

Several years before we set off on our Blue Zones adventure,

Dan had visited Singapore doing research for his happiness book. While there, and unbeknownst to me at the time, he had met my friend Greg, a Canadian commodity trader. A few years later, over coffee one morning, I told Greg about our plans for visiting the Blue Zones. "Oh my gosh, I know Dan! I'll introduce you!" he said.

Greg connected us via email, and prior to starting our travels, I dropped Dan a short note to thank him for providing the inspiration. We exchanged pleasantries and, after completing each country, I let him know that we had ticked another location off the list. Later, I wrote to him again, after coming across the so-called "longevity grass," the antioxidant-rich grass which grows like a weed on Okinawa's southern islands. The grass was already being marketed within Japan as a longevity supplement, and I suggested that I help organize a supply to him which he could sell under the Blue Zones brand. However, he rejected my proposal out of principle. First, he correctly pointed out that the grass is not in fact widely consumed by people in Okinawa, so it can hardly be considered a factor in Okinawan longevity. But more importantly, he felt that marketing a supplement, especially to Americans, would give a false sense of health and wellness, and thereby give people an excuse to avoid exercise and eating right. Although at the time I was a little upset that he had rejected my idea, I respect his position and believe he is correct in terms of how people can misuse supplements.

By now we had visited three of the five Blue Zones: Okinawa, Costa Rica, and Sardinia. Our next stop, however, would prove to be the purest and, in our view, most authentic Blue Zone.

Ikaria is one of Greece's 6,000 islands, and one which most people seem to have not heard of. Although it's not far from the mainland of Turkey, it's still fairly remote and has a relatively small population of about 7,000 people.

One must be intentional about reaching Ikaria. There are no daytrips from Athens (or Turkey), and regular flights to the island only operate during peak tourist season. The fastest ferry takes six hours from Athens and, as we would experience, weather can often mean ferries either don't sail or are delayed.

It's likely this remoteness has allowed the island to hold on to its cultural heritage. Also, the small population means it's simply not profitable for the likes of McDonald's to set up shop. Fast food has invaded all the other Blue Zones but is nowhere to be found on Ikaria.

After taking care of business in Bali and Singapore, we took a direct flight from Singapore to Athens. The weather makes late April to October the best time to visit Ikaria. It was now the second half of April, spring was in full swing and temperatures were warming. The Greek islands are well photographed in the summer months when the weather is warm and the sea is blue, but winter months are generally cold and rainy. We had waited as long as we could after winter before arriving in Greece to give us the best chance of avoiding inclement weather and, for the most part, the weather was good.

There are only a handful of hotels on Ikaria. Airbnb had about a hundred listings and, once again, we serendipitously managed to find a jewel of a place to stay. George and Eleni Karimalis's place is hailed on Airbnb as a "Traditional Ikarian Farmhouse" but it was so much more. For us, it was the only window we needed for the next two weeks to see and experience first-hand the most authentic Blue Zone lives of all our travels.

George and Eleni's home was a short drive from the ferry port of Evdilos, where we arrived from Athens. They own five hectares (about twelve acres) of certified organic farmland, most of which is used to grow grapes for the 14,000 bottles of wine they produce onsite each year.

The land has been in George's family for generations and some of the structures, now renovated and turned into guestrooms, are about five hundred years old. They are a working winery, farm, and hotel wrapped into one, hosting up to ten guests at a time. During our stay we would meet a number of guests, mostly from Europe and about half of whom seemed to make a regular habit of coming to Ikaria and exclusively staying with George and Eleni.

Both originally from Ikaria, George and Eleni actually met in Athens, as young adults. They had both left their homeland for university and then started careers there, Eleni as a nurse and George as an economist. They married and started a family and then, over twenty years ago, decided to move back to their native island. They wanted to raise their four children on Ikaria, their ancestral land. Their children are now adults and most have stayed on the island, producing multiple grandchildren in recent years. Family gatherings are frequent and full of life—great food, a bit of wine, and even dancing. At times it felt like we were on a movie set.

George and Eleni are, for the most part, self-sufficient in terms of what they grow. Chickens give them meat and eggs, goats give them milk (for cheese) and more meat, and a vegetable garden provides lots of greens. Beyond that, almost anything else which grows or is produced on the island they can barter for with wine. Honey, for example, is so prevalent on the island that George doesn't even bother with keeping bees. Each day we ate breakfast and dinner together with our hosts, and often with other guests too, and on several days also helped Eleni with the cooking. After ten days we really did *not* want to leave, and although we spent a few more days on other parts of the island, our stay with George and Eleni allowed us to experience all the key elements of Ikarian longevity.

Eleni's grandmother had lived to be exactly one hundred

years of age, so we'd come to a good place to learn something. George has the air of a typical Greek philosopher— skeptical and highly intellectual, which makes for interesting, and very entertaining, dinner conversation. He is a fountain of knowledge in almost any topic you can think of, and is incredibly passionate about wellness and eating (as well as drinking) for longevity. George and Eleni know Dan Buettner and one of Eleni's recipes is featured in a Blue Zone recipe book, *The Blue Zones Kitchen* (National Geographic, 2019).

Most people tend to assume, first and foremost, that a key longevity factor in any Blue Zone is the local diet. Dan asserts, in his writings, that people in the Blue Zones "tend to eat a plant-based diet." That may be slightly overstating the case, but after learning that Dan's life partner is an ardent proponent of the vegan lifestyle, it's not a surprise to me that this would influence the Blue Zone message. Although we didn't particularly notice a strong emphasis on plant-based diets in the locations we visited, there was one common food which did rank high on all the menus—beans.

Beans, of different varieties, showed up as a significant source of protein for Ikarians; as did fish (including octopus) and meat (mostly lamb/goat and chicken). The most common beans we ate were chickpeas and fava beans. Peas are also beans, with both technically falling into the category of legumes. Virtually all Ikarian protein sources—animals and legumes—are grown locally. This factor of eating local is more important for health, and the environmental, than eating a strict plant-based diet.

We ate what felt like a good balance between plant-based foods and animal products. Some days were meatless, others were not. The key, however, is that none of the animal protein we ate came from factory farms. This is easy enough to do on Ikaria, but much harder to do in densely populated cities or more developed countries. As a general rule, I strongly advocate eating a plant-based diet for myself and anyone living in the world of industrial food, which is pretty much the entire world nowadays.

It really is as simple as it sounds. Locally sourced food, prepared at home, is how almost everyone lived a hundred years ago, and processed foods (anything in a package) didn't exist. This is the Blue Zone way of eating and, in a place like Ikaria, it is still possible to eat this way without putting in a huge amount of effort. Back in Houston or Singapore, I shy away from meat, and lean toward plant-based. After our Blue Zone travels, Galina and I now eat more beans than we used to. They are a good substitute for meat and one of the three most important longevity elements which we identified as being common among the Blue Zones. Of course, this conclusion came about solely as a result of following a highly *un*scientific method of simply forming an opinion based on our own personal experiences.

***

God, beans, and a clear sense of purpose (a "why"), to me, sum up the most important factors that impact longevity. Also of note, a common geographical feature of all five of the Blue Zones is they are all near the sea, and all have varying degrees of rugged (hilly or mountainous) terrain. This may be largely coincidence, but there does seem to be an obvious health benefit. Hills result in regular cardio exercise, and especially so in the past when people had to walk from town to town, or up and down the hillsides to get goods or fish from the sea.

Ikaria has a history not dissimilar to that of Sardinia in that in centuries past people were safer in the hills. Until 1828, pirates were commonplace in the Aegean Sea, which sits between modern-day Turkey and Greece. Trade ships have sailed here for centuries, even in the days before Christ. The Apostle Paul sailed the Aegean on his missionary journeys and the Bible's Book of

Revelation was written on the Greek island of Patmos, which can be seen from Ikaria. All this movement of people and trade was a breeding ground for pirates and criminals of all sorts, but by 1828, the US Navy helped to rid the Aegean of them, after an American merchant ship had been attacked a few years earlier. The last two centuries have been considered pirate-free.

Because of the pirates, any houses built on Ikaria before 1828 were built up in the hills and without a normal chimney. Fires, for ovens and heating, were necessary in homes, but chimneys were made to diffuse the smoke through the cracks of the stone roof tiles, making them harder to be seen by invaders in the sea. George and Eleni's farm has one "no-chimney" building left, which has since been restored.

Civilization on Ikaria dates back to 7,000 BC and the island has managed to remain relatively isolated and self-sufficient over the years. This helped keep the gene pool strong; weaker members of the population died off before being able to reproduce, or at least being able to reproduce as much as the more able-bodied. This combination of isolation and a tough physical environment is common, to varying degrees, in all four of the Blue Zones we had visited to date. Before cars, people walked these rugged hills regularly as a normal part of life.

We walked a lot in Ikaria, both down to the sea and back up the hill to George and Eleni's house, about an hour each way. While Ikaria does not have the same kind of dramatic elevations as Sardinia, it is still a rocky and rugged island with its highest point measuring just over a thousand meters (vs. eighteen-hundred meters in Sardinia).

One day we decided to crash the weekly hike of the local hiking club, which we had found on Facebook. They were due to hike up from the coast to a small village square where they planned to meet for a simple lunch. We set out from a parking area and found our way by old and very rough roads. We passed beehives, goats, and the occasional local farmer who kept us pointed in the right direction. As we neared the destination village, we met a young Greek woman.

"How are you?" she said in a surprisingly American accent, which, of course, brought about questions.

Katerina was born in Ikaria, then moved to America as a child with her parents, but recently returned to her Ikarian roots in search of a more authentic and simple life. She accompanied us on the final stretch up the hill to the small village square. Other hikers arrived around the same time and we then set about erecting tables and benches for lunch. Because community events and festivals are so common, every village has its own permanent set of tables and benches on hand.

A few days later we bumped into yet another American who had returned to his roots. We were driving through a small village on the south side of the island and decided to stop to ask directions from one of the few humans we could find. The young man was getting into his car when I pulled up next to him to ask if I was heading in the right direction. I spoke slowly and liberally used hand gestures to make my point, assuming English was not his first language, but was shocked with his reply in a full-on American accent. He too had lived most of his life in the US and had recently returned to live connected to his roots on Ikaria. That night over dinner, George and Eleni confirmed that the young people we had met were not isolated cases but part of a small, yet growing trend on Ikaria of emigrants returning home. There is something magnetic about this island.

We were fortunate that the timing of our two-week stay on Ikaria corresponded with Easter. This gave us the chance to experience another one of the three Blue Zone commonalities— God. All Blue Zones have histories of committed religious practice, and with Easter upon us, we had a chance to join in.

The Greek Orthodox tradition is similar in many respects to that of the Russian Orthodox, as both are part of the Eastern Orthodox Church. From my personal experience in Russia and Eastern Europe, Orthodox churches take Easter quite seriously, more so than most churches in the West, where the focus is more on Christmas.

Ikaria's approach to Easter didn't disappoint. Churches on the island are as common as Baptist churches in Texas, the only difference being their sizes. There aren't any mega-churches on Ikaria like there are in Texas, most are small, some even tiny, which can hold maybe twenty people comfortably. Each village has its own church and priests serve multiple villages, staggering service times as the priest hops from village to village to conduct them. Easter calls for multiple services to take place nightly throughout the week leading up to the Easter weekend, with the two most important services being held on Good Friday and then the Saturday night at around midnight, leading into Sunday. The Saturday night service is the most dramatic. Words are spoken, prayers read, and incense burned prior to the congregation exiting the church building, and then proceeding to circle the church three times while singing and chanting.

Being part of a religious group, like any community group gathering around a common activity or cause, is a practical way of developing and maintaining human to human connections. It's these connections that play an important role in happiness and, it seems, longevity. As we grow older, our children create families and relationships of their own. But, even if our immediate families live nearby, family alone will likely not provide enough social interaction to satisfy our need for connection with others. Being active in a church can be a practical way to meet this basic need.

For many, participating in religious activity also supports a sense of cultural identity, and thus gives a feeling of belonging or being part of a tribe. But beyond the cultural and social aspects of being part of a religion, it seems to me that having belief in God, or a higher power, helps reduce some of the stress we create for ourselves. When we have the knowledge that there is more at play in our world than just what we do for a living, or what and who we identify ourselves as, life becomes easier to accept.

After our Blue Zone visits, I began to strongly encourage people to consider getting involved in some form of religious practice, even if they have doubts about some or all of the underlying belief systems. There is a very practical argument to be made that participation in religious groups improves longevity. Moreover, it is possible to separate one's religious practice from that of one's spiritual practice. For some these may be the same, whereas for others there may be overlap. Yoga and meditation, for example, can be described as spiritual practices and can be practiced separate from one's participation in a church or other religious group.

***

Starting in Okinawa, where our hosts spoke about their life purpose, their *ikigai*, we were struck by host after host, and others we met in the Blue Zones, who know what it is they are here to do with their lives each and every day. In Okinawa it was the dairy farmers who wanted to help the next generation connect with nature. In Costa Rica it was Hermida living on her small, self-sustaining coffee plantation, and whose daily activity was to serve her guests, her staff, and her family. "Hard work" at a family-owned bar in the mountains of Sardinia was the self-proclaimed secret there. On Ikaria, George and Eleni shared their way of life, their food, and their wine with the world. Sometimes it is the world coming to visit them as we did, but during the winter months they have, in recent years, gone "on tour" to the US and Europe to hold longevity and cooking workshops. They are living their *purpose* in life.

Alongside religion, Galina and I noted that Ikarians also have a strong cultural identity. We had previously read about Ikaria's parties, which are held mainly in the summer months. People gather in community halls and squares, using the same table and chairs we had used during lunch on our hike, to eat, drink, and dance. Ikarians travel from one village to another, depending on who they know. Foreign visitors are also welcomed.

Eleni insisted we join her at a party held in a nearby village on our last day on the island. We learned their dancing is serious business, going around in circles, hand in hand, for half an hour or more at a time is normal, although I needed a break after about fifteen minutes. There was grilled lamb, french fries, and homemade wine for sale, and we could see this was a great mechanism for Ikarians to fellowship together, much in the same way their ancestors have been doing for centuries.

The hikes, the food, and the authentic experiences we had living with George and Eleni allowed us to see the simplicity of life on Ikaria, the only Blue Zone we visited where we left feeling like we weren't yet ready to do so. We felt happy and at peace on this unique island in the Aegean Sea.

We might well be inclined to call the place "home" if it wasn't so difficult to reach, although that is a key factor in what makes Ikaria such a special place. Looking back, it was clear we had saved the best for last, although this was not intentional or expected. We came to Ikaria with no expectations of what we would find but left inspired and in love with this magical island.

***

With four Blue Zones now under our belts and less than

a month to go to our one-year anniversary of setting off from Singapore on this journey, we could see that getting in a visit to Loma Linda, California, America's sole Blue Zone, would be a challenge, at least within the one year we had given ourselves. And, frankly speaking, it just didn't seem to be calling ours names.

When I had read about the Seventh Day Adventist community and their healthy lifestyle, I concluded that Loma Linda had been included in the book to show a modern and, more importantly, American location to which American readers could potentially relate. This wasn't, of course something Dan Buettner ever admitted to, but at this point we were feeling as though we had accomplished our primary goal of seeing the core, and most certainly, the oldest Blue Zones.

Although the goal posts had moved along the way, and we had made some unplanned detours, we now felt that we had accomplished what we had set out to do.

What would come next was a different story.

Galina had, on our journey, proclaimed her desire to move to Paris and enroll in Le Cordon Bleu culinary school, the same school made famous by Julia Child. In time, we would come to realize that this was really a cry for some stability, after a year of wandering the world with no real longer-term vision or purpose for our lives. But we had experienced and learned a lot visiting the four Blue Zones, and it set the stage for us to get clear in the months to come about our relationship, and a shared vision for what we wanted from the second half of our lives—the final fifty years! Although unplanned, we could not ignore the symbolism of us both turning fifty during this year of travel, while learning from those in places where people lived to one hundred or more. We actually celebrated the advent of Galina's 50th birthday as we boarded the ferry in Evdilos, Ikaria, which then took us back to Athens. We stood on the pier in the cool night air, along with several hundred other departing passengers, waiting to board the large ship, just as midnight struck.

We both were now fifty. The ferry took us, overnight, to the Piraeus Port in Athens, where our sons, Nicholas and Marcus, waited to greet us as we arrived. The boys had flown to Athens the previous day to spend a few days with us and celebrate not only Galina's birthday, but also the completion of our Blue Zone explorations. This really was a special time to celebrate as a family.

Our travels were complete but there was so much now to distil. The key questions about who we were and what we wanted from the rest of our lives remained unanswered. It would take the best part of the next year for those answers to show up.

PREPARING FOR TAKE-OFF

"The greatest loss of all may be the diminished potential you experience when unplugged from your core."
- John G. Blumberg

EXACTLY ONE YEAR TO THE DAY after our departure from Singapore for Taiwan, en route to Okinawa, we were sitting in a restored mill, at the *Le Moulin des Quatre Saisons*, a Michelin-starred restaurant in La Flèche, France, ordering two glasses of Champagne as an aperitif for our celebratory lunch. This was our second time in the country, and one of fourteen countries we had visited in the past year. The Champagne arrived and, while proposing a toast to what would come next, I found myself feeling very emotional as I reflected on the year.

Because I didn't know what was to come next, my focus simply had to be on the past year and all that we'd experienced together. So many impactful locations, people, and events. Not only had we visited fourteen countries together and met so many interesting people, we had also both turned fifty, I had lost my father, and we had gained a grandchild. What a year it had been. Despite that, neither of us were any closer to being able to honestly answer the key existential questions about our relationship and what would come next. Our journey of discovery was not yet over.

We had no sense at all of where we would start to put down some roots. We had organized a summer of pet sits all over England, and from October Galina had enrolled herself in cooking school in Paris. Since I hadn't shown any leadership in crafting a future for us, Galina—in part out of frustration with me—had taken matters into her own hands.

I was not wild about the prospect of living in Paris and, in any case, I had Green School and other business that would need attending to in Asia. I could see that this French adventure may signal some fork in the road where we might each end up taking a different path. Only time would tell.

Over lunch we tried to talk about what would come next, but it was easier to simply reminisce about the past year. We might, of course, actually learn something from all we'd experienced anyway. One of the recurring themes I had noted in the Blue Zones was the concept of personal values. We had been shown repeatedly that people we had met seemed to hold certain concepts, or values, as key tenets of their lives—their core values. In Costa Rica we experienced *family* as a core value, in Sardinia it was *hard work*. In Okinawa our dairy farm hosts modeled *service* to others, and we saw how *religion* was a common core value in Ikaria.

But what were my core values? This was something that, in all my fifty years, I had never properly considered. So, over lunch I told Galina that I would do some "values work" in the months ahead to at least be clear about my grounding in life. Perhaps that would then help determine what would come next.

We finished our gourmet lunch together and both knew that, although neither of us were making plans to leave the relationship, we were yet to be clear and committed to each other for the long haul. Neither of us had a better alternative, and many couples stick together for that very reason, but our year of traveling had not magically brought us closer together as we'd hoped. We were, in fact, still quite close, but we both seemed to be sitting on the fence when it came to a decision about being truly committed to each other.

The next day I did some research and ordered a book, *Return on Integrity: The Individual's Journey to the One Essential Thing* by John G. Blumberg. John is, like me, a former partner with Arthur Andersen. He left his bean counting career, however, years ago to pursue a life as a writer and speaker. Although I've yet to meet him, his story was always inspirational to me and I've followed his works over the years. And it just so happened that his latest book was dedicated to helping people discover their core values. John's definition of integrity is when one lives in full alignment with one's core values. This sounded so simple and appealing, yet it was not something I could relate to, at least in that moment.

Being clear about your core values and then living in accordance with them requires intentional living. Although I had made many intentional, well-considered decisions about my life in the past, much of my life was characterized by reacting to circumstances. While there is nothing wrong with being opportunistic, in my life I seemed to have a consistent theme of reacting to various opportunities rather than purposefully pursuing what I wanted. The good news was that, despite this, I had managed to live an incredibly interesting life, married an amazing woman, and raised three lovely children. But at this mid-point in life, I was now feeling the desire to be clear about who I am and what that would mean for how I live.

So where to begin with core values? What were mine? I wasn't sure I knew, at least without doing some work to figure it out. In the weeks that followed, Blumberg's book took me on a journey into my soul to determine what values and key principles form the bedrock of who I am.

Blumberg defines a core value as "a principal state of being. It is the central, innermost, or most essential part of anyone."[vi] He makes the point that any of our needs, desires and wants can usually be traced to a core value by asking the question "why?"—usually up to five times. Keep asking yourself "why?" and you'll eventually get to the answer "just because." It's here that you have most likely identified a core value.

A few examples from my own life: I started with the big one for me—money. Throughout my life, why have I always wanted to earn a lot of money? "To avoid financial failure" would have been my initial response, even though I'm not sure what would be defined as being a financial failure. This was not a core value but rather a *fear*. Fears can be good motivators to take action, but I went back to the key question: "Why do I want to earn a lot of money?"

"To buy things" or "to feel successful" came up, but again this begged the question of "why?"

In the end I identified a core value of *independence* as being at the heart of why I wanted to earn money. If one is intentional with it, money brings optionality to life and can provide a large degree of financial independence. A further key question to ask is how much is enough, and setting clear goals around that. Otherwise, it's easy to fall into the trap of greed and simply living by the mantra that more is better. With such a mentality we never get off the wheel of chasing money, and this is certainly something which I had been guilty of in the past. I had earned millions, yet was determined that I should earn tens of millions. During that time, I never once sat down to really ask myself how much I needed to be financially independent. Although it transpires that independence is one of my core values, I was not connected to that value and hence was living without integrity.

By coming to this realization, I was able to quickly assess my life, my wants and needs, and quantify what combination of income and net worth I needed, both now and in the future, to feel financially independent. Easy. With that answer, I could start to chart a course to a clear goal and then live in accordance with my core value. Knowing the "why" makes all the difference.

To me, independence also meant not feeling as though I had to work for a company, and this helped explain why I had been happily working for myself for the past decade. In this case, and although I had not been consciously aware of it, I was living according to my core value.

Another value I was able to realize during my work was that of *sharing* with others. This is the teacher in me, the person who has consistently desired to share skills, ideas and lessons learned, with others. More than sharing things or money, this is about sharing myself with the world. Whether it be through coaching, or writing this book, my desire to share and improve the lives of others is core to who I am. The good news is that I was already living this core value to a large degree, but now I can be even more intentional about it.

There were other core values I uncovered, including *adventure*. Once again, this has shown up in me since I was a child in things like building forts and treehouses in the woods, and venturing out on my bicycle to places I'd never been. Given my adult history of moving to Russia at the age of twenty-three, and all the intrepid travels which followed, plus, of course, our recent Blue Zone adventures, it is safe to say this was a value I had lived by pretty well.

It took longer, however, to come to terms with my final two final core values, and these were the two which would allow Galina and me to address the key questions surrounding our life together now as empty nesters. There are many things in life which we simply have to go through before finding our way out, and in this respect Galina and I would need to hit rock bottom before we could come out victorious on the other side.

***

With our Michelin-starred one-year anniversary lunch in France behind us, we set off for a pet-sitting summer in England. We began by taking care of two ponies in Lancashire, moved on to dogs and cats in various homes around London, and finished up in a beautiful home in the southwest county of Devon. The home was a five-minute walk from the South West Coast Path, England's longest official footpath. It covers 630 miles of often rugged coastline, starting in Somerset, near Wales, and then traversing the coasts of Devon, Cornwall, and Dorset.

I had recently learned about the South West Coast Path from reading *The Salt Path*[vii], a book by British author Raynor Winn. It tells the story of how she and her husband suddenly found themselves homeless in their early 50s, so it was no accident that I had bought this book. As a way to take action and create forward momentum in their lives, Winn and her husband spent two years hiking the entire 630-mile path, wild camping and living off government welfare payments. A friend of ours recommended it to me after hearing us complain about our feeling "homeless" during our global travels. Although the circumstances surrounding their homelessness were quite different to ours (they had lost all they owned in a lawsuit from a bad business deal), there were some insights shared by the author with which I could relate.

They had discovered that while hiking, when they told strangers along the way they had lost all they owned and were simply now hiking the path, they almost always received a cold and distant response. The conversation would end quickly as they were looked at as either lower class or dangerous. However, if they tweaked their story in just the slightest way to say that they were simply hiking the entire trail as a big adventure, they were somehow heralded as inspirational heroes. This was generally the response we had received from people we'd met in the past year simply because we were able to, honestly, frame our story as one of choice and abundance. While we felt blessed and grateful for that, we were in many ways just as lost and confused about what to do with our lives as Raynor and her husband were as they hiked the Path.

Their story had been key in inspiring me to write about our journey, and it felt fun for me that we got the chance to finish up our summer in a house minutes away from the South West Coast Path. Even if we only got to hike it for a few miles, it was an inspirational way to conclude our time together in England.

We had spent more than three months in England, killing time before our move to Paris, yet neither of us were any closer to figuring out what we wanted in terms of our relationship and what our lives as empty nesters were going to look like. We would alternate between moments of tension and arguments and a legitimate peace. In general, there was more peace than war, and functionally we got along very well together, but there was also an unspoken frustration that neither of us were willing to commit to being truly together as one in this new season of life.

***

The Salt Path takes its title from the author's observation on the hike that wild blackberries growing along the path take in salt from the ocean air, and thus have a very slight taste of salt to them. I had read the book before our first walk along the path together, which just so happened to take place at a difficult time for us. I don't remember the nature of the argument, but in our relationship we were certainly at war that day. Some harsh words were spoken by each of us and we ended up hiking for some time separated by about 30 meters, with Galina running off in front. It was September, and still blackberry season in England, and after a while Galina came across a patch. We'd been enjoying wild blackberries on walks throughout the summer so stopping for a snack was standard procedure. By the time I caught up, Galina had already been eating berries for a few moments. She said to me, in a nonchalant, matter-of-fact way, "You can taste salt in these berries."

"*What!*" I exclaimed. "How did you know that?" as if I had been the only person with the sacred knowledge of the salt-infused berries. I angrily accused her of having read the book. She hadn't, and I had never bothered to share how the name of the book came about. My anger came from a jealousy that she had been able to so quickly pick up on this subtle nuance of South West Coast Path blackberries. Seeing through my anger, however, I also held her in high regard for her exquisite tasting ability, especially since, if I were being honest, I couldn't taste any salt at all. To me they were just blackberries.

My bubble popped; I didn't know how to react. I was angry and jealous, while simultaneously in awe of her and that she was so aware and in tune with nature. How many other times over the years had she simply known or been right about something based on intuition?

Many . . . and the truth of that hurt. Either way, this unexpected interaction with salty blackberries had managed to reunite us on the hike, and we enjoyed a few handfuls together while they lasted. Summer was coming to an end and a new season, in Paris, was about to begin.

I did, however, feel like I was moving to Paris under duress. I did not want to study French, had been brainwashed as a child that Paris was full of rude Parisians ("Paris is lovely, except for the French," my dad used to say), and saw no practical reason for me to be there. Also, my business with Green School back in Bali was now demanding more of my time, as were our international expansion plans. I had basically decided that I would tolerate the place while Galina did her cooking course, but that I'd also be coming and going on business trips for work, which I clearly valued more than our current relationship.

Galina, on the other hand, had begun a love affair with Paris and the French language before we even got there. For the past six months, she had been studying French online, both self-study and with a tutor on Skype, and was almost fluent by the time we got off the train at Paris' Gare de Lyon station. The plan was to be based in Paris for about a year and a half while Galina completed various levels and courses at Le Cordon Bleu. To me this felt like an eternity, but at the same time I wasn't willing to offer any alternative. In any case, Galina had pre-paid for all the courses so there was really no backing out at this point. I would suffer through this phase and was planning to travel back and forth between Paris and Asia as necessary to do my job, although hopefully not so much that it damaged our marriage. At least that is what I told myself.

In truth, the marriage was already in a dangerous place, and my travels were not about to help matters.

We had been in Paris just ten days when my first trip came to fruition. I needed to fly to New York to meet with our Green School partners from Mexico and resolve a few disagreements. Two days there did the trick, and I then flew down to Houston to pay a surprise visit to our daughter, grandchildren, and my mother for the weekend. From Houston I flew to Bali, where I spent about ten days before returning to Paris. I had completely circumnavigated the globe in about two weeks.

Once back in Paris, Galina and I did the best we could to avoid conflict. Deep down, Galina wanted me with her there for the eighteen months of her studies, and for us to be together *living* (not homeless) in one place. That, after all, had been the main reason she'd even signed up for the Le Cordon Bleu classes—to create stability for us. I, on the other hand, still had my dragons to slay and did not feel the need to prioritize Galina's plans. This left us both hurt and angry, not a good combination of ingredients for a successful empty nest stage of marriage. Or any stage of marriage for that matter.

But before we could even deal with the hurt and anger, I hit the road yet again. I hadn't been back in Paris more than two weeks before I left for India. John Hardy had invited me to attend a conference there, along with some other friends and colleagues from Bali, and to then spend about a week traveling around Rajasthan. Had it not been for her studies, Galina would have joined me, but since that wasn't an option and I really wanted to visit this unique part of the world, I went alone.

India lived up to expectations in terms of dirt, dust, and chaos. Cows roam the streets while cars and 3-wheeled auto rickshaws are in constant motion. Over the course of a week we visited Jaipur, Bikaner, and Jaisalmer.

Jaipur, the capital of Rajasthan, is famous for its arts and crafts, as well its gems and jewelry. John, a former jeweler who knows India well, took me to a friendly source for fine jewelry. I picked out several nice Christmas gifts for Galina, the least I could do having abandoned her in Paris. Although they would be well received a few weeks later, they, of course, did nothing to get to the core of the problem. Diamonds may be some girls' best friend, but Galina was wanting her *real* best friend back with her—both physically and emotionally.

A few months earlier, while in England, Galina and I had listened to the audio-book version of Dr. Marshall B. Rosenberg's *Nonviolent Communication: A Language of Life.*[viii] In it, an entire framework is set out for resolving conflict through empathic listening aimed at understanding the underlying need of the other party. According to Wikipedia's summary of nonviolent communication, Rosenberg holds the view that most conflict between individuals or groups arises from miscommunication about their human needs, due to coercive or manipulative language that aims to induce fear, guilt, shame, etc. These "violent" modes of communication, when used during. conflict, divert the attention of the participants away from clarifying their needs, their feelings, their perceptions, and their requests, thus perpetuating the conflict.

As we listened to the book together, we saw how each of us failed to adequately express, to each other, our core needs and desires in our relationship. We weren't yet ready to do the hard work necessary to really address the core issues, but the seeds were being sown. Maintaining the status quo in our relationship had simply been the path of least resistance. Galina had insisted we move to Paris for her to attend Le Cordon Bleu, not because she wanted to become a professional chef, but because in her heart she was longing for a place to call home for more than a few weeks. On the other hand, I had not been clear about my professional needs which, for now at least, meant spending time in Bali and other potential Green School locations around the world. Each of us was confused about what the other person wanted, or were unwilling to accept it. So, for the time being, we had made our bed and we had to sleep in it. It felt that, for now, we were stuck.

This dynamic continued over the weeks leading up to the Christmas holidays. Despite rising tensions not being addressed, we muddled along and would enjoy a respite for a few weeks over Christmas and New Year when our boys came to stay. We spent a few days together in Paris before Christmas, then rented a car and drove down to Slovenia for most of the time together. It was a bit of trip down memory lane for all four of us as we had lived there together a decade earlier. We rang in the new year standing on Ljubljana's main square while local celebrities and a rock band performed on a temporary stage. Despite being surrounded by revelers and most of my family, as the new year started I felt alone and confused. I did my best to put my arm around Galina and we exchanged a lukewarm kiss at the stroke of midnight. Still faking it.

I knew that I didn't want to carry on this way for the second half of my life.

Back in Paris, with the boys back at school—Marcus in London and Nicholas in Mexico about to start a semester abroad— we were now alone having to face our demons and decide, once and for all, what we wanted from each other, and what we wanted to create, or not, in a relationship together.

***

I usually fall asleep quite quickly and can manage to sleep throughout the night, even when I'm under stress. But for the first time I can remember, I was not sleeping well. For virtually all of our married life we had consistently said the words "I love you" before falling asleep. In recent months, however, we had not. Galina had the courage to acknowledge this and said she wasn't even sure what it meant, and why bother saying it simply out of routine? Of course, she knew what it meant; she just wasn't feeling it anymore.

This acknowledgement of the state of our relationship was wearing on me. We would speak about the future with no sense of certainty and I was not providing any direction or leadership regarding what *our* future would hold. I was stuck in fear of what might or might not happen and the infinite number of "what if" scenarios which might, or might not, make Galina happy. Her happiness, or rather my perceived notions of what would make her happy, were more important to me than my own vision for our lives, or what would make me happy. Tension was building to a point that something had to give.

Finally, after a night of very little sleep (for either of us it seemed) and no words being spoken between us, the time had come. I got out of bed as the sun rose and instinctively grabbed my laptop and started to type out a letter to Galina with the following opening line:

> I love you—as I know best how to love, which isn't perfect, I know…

I went on to acknowledge that money has and does cloud my vision, offering an excuse, of sorts, as to why I had not set out a clear vision for the years to come in our relationship. The final two core values on my list, family and dedication, were, at last, driving me to a point of firm reconciliation and decisiveness in our relationship. I wanted to stay together in a relationship where we love each other, and I wanted to be loved in return. I wanted compassion and friendship to be the hallmark of our relationship, not resentment and anger.

I apologized for how things had worked out with Paris. I had messed up her dream of us living together in the "City of Light," leaving her alone there regularly while I chased my own dreams. I asked for forgiveness and that we work together to work through this season.

Next, at long last, I proceeded to set out a vision for our life together in the coming decades. I believed this would have us living together in Asia (where my work is centered) in the near future, having a base and owning a home in Europe, and eventually moving back to Texas to finish our life together near our daughter. Of course, details could change due to circumstances, including the possibility of children moving, but I was finally willing to articulate a vision for the future . . . and a future together. Any doubt of whether I wanted to stay with Galina or not was gone.

I had suddenly taken ownership of two remaining core values—*family* and *dedication*—that, for some reason, I had been reluctant to acknowledge until that moment.

As I was writing my letter, Galina had gotten out of bed and was at work on her computer in our small Paris kitchen. Neither of us had spoken a word to each other about what we were doing. Once I'd finished composing my message to Galina I walked into the kitchen and, still without speaking, handed her my computer.

And she handed me hers.

She had also expressed what her heart was feeling in a letter, although she had taken a slightly different tack. Galina's was not simply a letter from her to me. It was from me to her—revealing what *she* needed to hear from her husband.

The message, which she had written on her computer in my voice, went like this:

No words can express the gratitude I feel when I think of you. I know it has been a bumpy road, especially recently, but I take full responsibility for it. I also acknowledge and love the fact that you value other things in life more than what money can buy. I am so grateful for your understanding of my work situation and how much I like it, and for allowing me to do it (maybe not so graciously as I would have wanted) but I take it happily and thank you for allowing me to chase my dreams and ambitions. I will do my best to make your life as pleasant and happy as possible because that is what you deserve and what makes my life worthy on this earth.

I know we cannot be physically together sometimes but who said we cannot be together energetically . . . I will think of you and pray for us every day. I will start and end my day with the gratitude that God put us together. Maybe I will even write you a letter or send you a song or a playlist of love songs to say how much I love you and am blessed to have you in my life. With each song you can imagine, just how I did when I listened to it, how we're gonna dance when we are old (and that will happen in a blink of an eye).

I am honored to have you to be with me in this slow and sometimes painful process. I am forever grateful.

Although I had not written those words, they were an accurate reflection of my heart. Tears filled our eyes as we read the letters each of us had just penned.

We didn't say much to each other. I think we were in awe that we had somehow managed to both take steps toward reconciliation simultaneously and using very similar means. I reached for my iPhone, and pressed play on one of our favorites—Ed Sheeran's *Thinking Out Loud*.

We danced together in the small space of that Paris kitchen for the next few minutes, with tears streaming down both our faces.

It was not as though we now had all the answers to what would come next. We didn't. And little did we know that, within a few weeks, a new virus from China, COVID-19, would impact any and all plans we had previously made.

***

So, what about those two remaining core values—family and dedication? Well, they had clearly made themselves known to me that morning in Paris as we danced together.

Although I may be stating the obvious, family *is* important to me. With Natasha having been a key fixture in our two years of dating, Galina and I had started our family even before we were married, and Nicholas was born just sixteen months after. I had always loved my family and done my best to make them a priority. Even though the "kids" were now all adults and out of the house, I still had a family. It had even been growing and, Lord willing, will continue to grow in the years to come. In our Blue Zone travels we had come face to face with the core value of family time and again. I had seen it in action and even felt it, but it was not yet a value that I had consciously and intentionally acknowledged until that moment. It's as if it was sitting right under my nose the entire time.

Related to my own core value of family sits the core value of dedication. It is simply who I am. While there is a potential dark side to dedication (being "dedicated to a fault" can lead me to letting others treat me like a doormat), in a healthy relationship I am a dedicated and trusted friend or partner.

Living with integrity means living in accordance with one's core values. These were the final pieces of the values puzzle to fall into place for me. The lingering questions of the recent years had been clearly answered in our kitchen that morning in Paris. I now knew that Galina and I were going to stay married and build our lives together. Exactly what our joint life would look like was a story yet to be written, but I was confident those details would fall into place in due course.

A few weeks later, I got a chance to put my newfound core values into practice. It was the end of February 2020 and the COVID-19 virus had the world concerned. People had been dying in China and there were talks of isolated outbreaks in some villages in Spain and Italy. But the real crisis had not yet begun. I had spent the day in London, where I had some work-related meetings, and I was scheduled to fly to Paris and change planes for a flight to Bali. My flight from London was late getting into Paris' Charles De Gaulle airport, so I had to run through the airport, changing terminals, to make the flight to Bali on time. I was one of the last passengers to board the plane, and a flight attendant took my coat in exchange for a glass of Champagne, as

I flopped into my seat. I quickly took out my phone and called Galina to let her know I'd made the tight connection and that my plane was about to take off.

"Do you really have to fly?" she asked me. *Oh my gosh, why was she asking me this now?* "I don't think you should go," she continued.

At this time only a few countries had closed their borders, including the United States, and only to passengers from China, so the potential of getting stuck somewhere, much less sick from the virus, was not yet on my mind.

"There is just a lot of uncertainty right now and I really don't want to risk you getting stuck somewhere with me here alone in France," Galina said. I knew I had very little time to make a decision.

"Okay," I said. "Let me see if I can get off." I quickly hung up the phone, jumped up and walked to the galley, where the plane door was still open. "Can I get off this flight?" I asked the same attendant who had just poured my Champagne. Slightly startled, she asked what the problem was, and I explained simply that I had changed my mind about this trip and that I wanted to go home. A minor commotion erupted between the flight attendants as they radioed to the check-in staff that I wanted to disembark. Fortunately, I had not checked in any luggage. I was hurriedly given back my coat and took my carry-on bag from the overhead compartment, as confused passengers, a few in masks, looked on. I was then escorted back down the jetway and an agent opened the terminal door, which had already been locked, and let me out.

Walking back through the airport, which I had just ran through less than thirty minutes before, was a bit surreal. I now walked slowly, thinking about the work implications of the meetings I would miss, but at the same time I felt a strong inner peace. I had made a decision which put my family—and more specifically

Galina—first. My actions had proven my dedication to Galina over my work. A firm decision based on my core values.

I was living with integrity.

I called Galina to tell her that I was coming home and, as I write this more than six months later, we have not been apart since. Life was not going to let us be separated any time soon. Less than three weeks after getting off that flight, France, and then all of Europe, closed its borders and instituted harsh lockdown measures.

A few weeks later, our son, Marcus, joined us in Paris. He'd traveled from London, where his university was being closed due to the virus. We lived together in our two-bedroom apartment for the next few months. Fortunately, we were allowed outside of the apartment once a day for exercise, and once a day to do some shopping, so long as we stayed within one kilometer (.62 of a mile) of our home.

One evening, a few weeks into the lockdown, Galina and I reflected on the timing of our reconciliation and recommitment to our relationship. Who knows what would have happened had we found ourselves locked in our apartment for months, living under the same roof but as disconnected from each other as we had previously been?

As I write this, exactly how the world will change after the COVID-19 pandemic remains to be seen. How will communities in the Blue Zones fare? My guess is that their relative isolation and strong immune systems will mean minimal disruption and few premature deaths.

As for us, we have begun to chart out a *plan de vida* for the coming years together. For the time being, Galina has put her Le Cordon Bleu studies on hold. Courses can be finished in the future at her own pace and are even available in other countries. We purchased an apartment in Valencia, building on our official residency in Spain, and this has fulfilled at least part of the vision set out a few months earlier in my letter to Galina. It has given us a *home*—a place on the map where we can spend time in between work and other travels, or to endure another lockdown if necessary. And it has given us at least some sense of rooting.

Our children, and grandchildren, are all spread around the world - in Texas, England and Spain – at least for now. We have yet to resolve our long-term desire to be in a community, along with multiple generations of family members, but how, when, and where that will happen will become clear in time. We can't expect to have all the answers now.

"Tomorrow is tomorrow," Masako had once told me in Okinawa.

I won't be flying alone *anywhere* anytime soon, and that makes me happy. We are fortunate to be in great health and to have the freedom to travel the world together, feeling at home wherever we happen to find ourselves. Our kids may have all flown from the nest, but our nest is still full of love and life as we continue to fly together, making new dreams come true.

We hold our dreams and goals lightly, however, and just as we did in the Blue Zones—together—we continue to let the details unfold on their own along on the way.

Here's to another fifty years together.

EPILOGUE

The impacts of the COVID-19 pandemic continued to play out in 2020 and into 2021 as this book went to print. We were fortunate to have our youngest son, Marcus, move in with us to our Paris apartment just as the world, including France, went into full lock-down in March 2020. I know we will always look back on that time together with fond memories. We enjoyed each other's company with French wine and cheese while watching how the pandemic started to impact the world from financial markets to the 'Black Lives Matter' movement sparked by the death of George Floyd, to the daily real-time death count on CNN.

By the summer, we were able to travel again, at least within Europe, and we managed to visit Ikaria, our favorite Blue Zone, one more time. We stayed with our friends George and Eleni for two weeks and believe that we may finally have found a place which we will return to time and again in the years to come.

As the year progressed we began to see a picture emerging for how our new life together would start to look. It would be a life of learning and adventure, with at least one shared passion that would serve as the new "glue" for our relationship. While settling down in one location remains somewhat elusive, the creative process of creating a home together is exciting. At the time of this writing in 2021, we are in the process of building new homes in Valencia, Spain and Bali, Indonesia. Creating comfortable and functional spaces allows us to dream and build something together which we can then share with the world. We are creating homes where we can invite friends for a meal, or which we can pass on to another family.

In late 2020 we moved to Bali to be closer to Green School. Owing to the pandemic, it became apparent that both the Bali school and the international network would need new investment to survive for the long-term. In May 2021, I closed a transaction with a strategic investor to secure Green School's future funding. I stepped down as chairman of the board and handed control to our new partner, freeing me up to begin a new stage in life.

I reflect on my core values often, and use them as a guide to determine how I am living my life and where I focus my energy. Getting off course at times is inevitable, but with *family* topping the list we have managed to have all three of our children, and our three grandchildren, spend extended periods of time with us in Bali during 2021. Galina and I have been intentional about creating these experiences, living out this shared core value together.

As I write this, it's been well over a year since we renewed our relationship in the Paris kitchen. For us, the kitchen is a central hub of a home so it is somewhat ironic and appropriate that such a significant life event took place in the kitchen. Neither of us have since wavered or doubted the recommitment we made to each other that day. We know who we are and have found our new glue.

Endnotes

[i] Dan Buettner, The Blue Zones: Lessons for Living Longer From the People Who've Lived the Longest (National Geographic, 2010).

[ii] https://www.bluezones.com/exploration/nicoya-costa-rica/

[iii] Available at: https://payhip.com/b/SGnj

[iv] Source: https://www.nationalgeographic.com/travel/world-heritage/petra-jordan/

[v] Bob Buford, Halftime: Practical Wisdom for Your Second Half (Grand Rapids, MI, Zondervan, 2015).

[vi] John Blumberg, Return on Integrity: The Individual's Journey to the One Essential Thing (Naperville, IL: Key Concepts, Inc, 2019), 34.

[vii] Raynor Winn, The Salt Path (Penguin, 2019)

[viii] Marshall B. Rosenberg, Nonviolent Communication: A Language of Life (Encinitas, CA: PuddleDancer Press, 2015).

Made in the USA
Columbia, SC
22 September 2021